ALLEN JACKSON

UNLEASHING THE POWER OF THE
HOLY SPIRIT

BOUND TRANSCRIPTS
SERMONS IN BOOK FORM

© 2019 by Allen Jackson
ISBN 978-1-61718-047-7

Published by Allen Jackson Ministries™
P.O. Box 331042 / Murfreesboro TN 37133-1042
allenjackson.com

Printed in the United States of America

TABLE OF CONTENTS

AN INTRODUCTION TO THE BOUND TRANSCRIPTS

The contents of this book are taken directly from the transcripts of Pastor Allen Jackson's sermons, in the order they were presented at World Outreach Church in Murfreesboro, Tennessee.

In bringing them to book form, our primary objective was to maintain the full integrity of the message, as it was delivered in the sanctuary. This means that for the overwhelming majority of the text, it is a verbatim transcription. In sections where the oral presentation didn't translate effectively to written word, only minor edits were made to reduce confusion for the reader.

Also, from time to time in the text you'll see paragraphs written in blue letters. These are sections where Pastor Allen has interjected an aside, or added a few extra thoughts to the idea after the sermon was delivered.

These sermons contain powerful and timeless truths from Scripture. We hope you enjoy reading them, and trust that as you choose to cooperate with the Spirit of the Lord, He will unleash freedom, peace, strength, love, hope, forgiveness, and restoration in your life.

God bless you on your journey.

• SERMON 1 •

I. WELCOMING THE HOLY SPIRIT

I want to begin a study with you under the general theme of unleashing the power of the Holy Spirit, but it's really an idea against a much larger idea, and that's believing God for a breakthrough in our lives. It's a universal need. We all have places where only God's involvement can bring about an outcome that's acceptable.

You know, I'm grateful for doctors. I believe in hard work and ingenuity and diligence and self-discipline and all of those things that are a necessary part of a healthy and whole life. But at the end of the day, life presents challenges to us that only God's involvement can bring about a satisfactory outcome. We need a breakthrough. And it seems that every time I sit down with a new set of lessons, they're another component in that larger idea. With this lesson I think that is uniquely true as well—that for a breakthrough in our lives we need to understand the Person of the Holy Spirit and what He affords us if we can cooperate with Him. The Holy Spirit is a person. So I'd like to craft the study and the context of this notion of unleashing the power of the Spirit of God in our lives, because it requires some responses from us for God's power to be made evident.

Now one of the principles that's clear in Scripture from the beginning of the story to the conclusion of the Book is that the power of God and the Person of the Holy Spirit are inseparable—they're almost synonymous. I'll give you an example. You know this verse by heart—first verse of the Bible. How does the Bible begin? "In the beginning..." You're so clever. "In the beginning God created the heavens and the earth, and the earth was void without shape..." And in verse 2 it says, "The Spirit of God hovered over the face of the deep"—that the Spirit of God was present for the creative power of God to be released in giving shape and order to the world in which we live. It begins in the first verses of Genesis, and it carries right through the entire Bible.

I tell you that because we have a tendency in organized religious context to somehow diminish the Person of the Holy Spirit. Now I don't know exactly why that it is, but we quibble about the assignments that we will welcome Him to, or the role that we imagine He can occupy. The reality in Scripture is that the Holy Spirit and the creative power of God are synonymous.

It's the Holy Spirit, the Bible tells us, that oftentimes delivered the Israelites from their enemies—sometimes whole armies of enemies—sometimes in more individual ways. It was the Holy Spirit that came upon Elijah the prophet and enabled him to outrun the chariots of Ahab across the Jezreel Valley. We're told that the Holy Spirit came upon the prophets, and they prophesied of what God would do in their generation and the generations to come. In the New Testament when the angel came to Mary with the announcement of the birth of the Son of God, Mary said, "How can this be?" And the angel said, "The Spirit of Most High God will overshadow you." The language is very similar to the Genesis narrative, "The creative power of God will come upon you."

Over and over throughout the story of Scripture the Holy Spirit is the Person through whom the power of God is made evident in our lives. You will not thrive or flourish as a Christ-follower apart from the Person of the Holy Spirit. So I'd like to begin our study with the simplest of ideas on welcoming the Holy Spirit into our lives, and I'll give you just two or three verses to help underscore the notion.

A. HOLY SPIRIT AND POWER

In Judges 14 in verse 6, there's a comment about Samson, one of the Judges. Samson is the strongman in the Bible. It says,

> *The Spirit of the LORD came upon him in power so that he tore the lion apart with his bare hands as he might have torn a young goat.*

JUDGES 14:6

Now without the Bible I wouldn't have known it was easy to tear a young goat apart with your bare hands. Apparently a lion is a far more difficult task, and Samson could only achieve that with the help of the Holy Spirit.

In fact the phrase is used repeatedly in Samson's life—that the Spirit of God would come upon him, and then he would demonstrate these feats of remarkable strength. He would pick up the gates of a city and carry them away. He could take the jawbone of a donkey and overcome a whole contingent of foreign soldiers. He had this remarkable strength when the Spirit of God would come upon him.

The Holy Spirit provided Samson with great strength. However, Samson was responsible for the formation of his character. Because He did not give attention to his character formation, he suffered and all Israel suffered. Demonstrations of the Spirit do not indicate good character or spiritual maturity.

Now his enemies were perplexed; when they looked at Samson they didn't understand the secret of his strength. That's why the whole Delilah initiative got launched. They wanted to know what the secret of his strength was. He finally told her of the covenant that had been made and the source of his strength—

and while he was asleep, she shaved his hair. You know the story. This produces one of the more tragic statements in the Bible — it says,

> *Then she called, "Samson, the Philistines are upon you!" He awoke from his sleep and thought, "I'll go out as before and shake myself free." But he did not know that the Lord had left him.*
>
> JUDGES 16:20

The presence of the Holy Spirit in your life is a good thing. You want to welcome Him.

Let's look at another verse. This time is Jesus' life, in Luke chapter 4 and verse 14 it says,

> *Jesus returned to Galilee in the power of the Spirit, and news about him spread through the whole countryside.*
>
> LUKE 4:14

Now at this point Jesus is thirty years old. He has lived for thirty years in almost total anonymity. He has no ministry; no one knows who He is. They think He's Mary and Joe's boy. He's just minding His own business, doing His own thing, and at the age of thirty He goes to the Jordan River to John the Baptist. He's baptized and at His baptism you'll remember that the Holy Spirit descended upon Jesus in the form of a dove. God said,

"This is my Son. I'm pleased with Him," and from that point forward for three years Jesus goes public.

That's when the supernatural part of Jesus' life begins—or certainly the miraculous part of His life. The healings begin, the deliverance from unclean spirits begins, He walks on the water, He opens blind eyes, He stands in the cemetery and calls out a dead man, and the man stumbles out of the tomb. All of those things followed the descent of the Spirit in Jesus' life. If Jesus needed the help of the Holy Spirit to accomplish God's purposes for His life, to let the power of God be unleashed in His life, I would submit that you and I most certainly do.

Now I'll give you one more passage:

For God did not give us a spirit of timidity, but a spirit of power, love and of self-discipline.

2 TIMOTHY 1:7

There's an association being made between the presence of the Spirit of God, and again, the power of God. They go together. So if we have need of a breakthrough—if we're inviting God into our lives, the best pathway forward, as I understand it, is an invitation to the Person of the Holy Spirit. You want to cooperate with Him. The Spirit of God is not timid. He's not frightened. Some translations say, "He hasn't given us a spirit of fear, but a spirit of power." There is an authority in the Spirit of God.

B. HOLY SPIRIT IN YOU

Now there's another aspect of this that's worth noting, and that has to do with the proximity of the Holy Spirit to your life. Is He distant? Is He far removed? In 1 Corinthians 6:19 it says, "Do you not know..."

We've learned by now that when you see that statement, what's the answer to the question? Right, probably not. Let's look at the full scripture.

Do you not know that your body is a temple of the Holy Spirit, who is in you, whom you have received from God? You are not your own; you were bought at a price. Therefore honor God with your body.

1 CORINTHIANS 6:19-20

"Do you not know that your body is a temple of the Holy Spirit?" Now the language is very simple. We can understand the meaning of the words, but the magnitude of the statement I think is a little bit lost on us.

For a thousand years the Hebrew people had, in the center of their life, a place of worship—initially the Tabernacle and then the Temple—and at the center of both of those structures was the Holy of Holies. This was the most sacred place on earth to the Hebrew people because it was said that in the Holy of Holies, the Spirit of God dwelt in the midst of His people. It was a tangible reminder that they were God's people and that He dwelt in their midst. It was in the Holy of Holies where the Ark of the Covenant was kept.

Now by the time we get to the first century and to Jesus' days, the Temple in Jerusalem was a magnificent structure. Herod the Great had renovated the Second Temple and expanded the Temple platform. It was one of the most magnificent structures in all of the Roman Empire. Tens of thousands of pilgrims came every year—non-Jewish pilgrims—just to see the Temple in its magnificence. Certainly for the Israelites it was the center of their national life. It was the grandest building in the nation. It was not only the center of worship for them, it was their national bank. It was the center of their political activity. It was the symbol of their power and authority. It unified them as a people, because in the center of the Temple was the presence of God.

And then when Jesus died on the cross something happened. Do you remember? Jesus' last words were, "Father into Your hands I commit my spirit." It says that the sky grew dark; the sun wasn't shining—that there was an earthquake, that many of the tombs in Jerusalem were split open, and the dead were raised to life. It says that in the Temple, the curtain that separated the Holy of Holies from the next court was torn in two from the top to the bottom.

And now Paul writes, "Don't you know that your body is the temple of the Holy Spirit? It's not that magnificent structure that Herod the Great oversaw. It took forty years to build. Your body is a temple of the Spirit of God. That the Spirit of the Living God dwells in you." That's a staggering statement. It truly is.

In John's Gospel, Jesus said that you couldn't participate in the Kingdom of God unless you're born again. When you make that profession of faith, it says that you become a totally new creation. In the same way God created Adam, shaped him from the dust of the ground, and breathed into him making him a living being, the Spirit of God is breathed into you and you become alive spiritually. The Holy Spirit lives in you. Do you recognize the dignity that brings to you?

Imagine the Spirit of Almighty God choosing you. And being present within you to help you overcome every challenge or weakness. That's a tremendous expression of God's love for you!

That's what Paul is saying. He says, "Glorify God. Honor God with your body. He lives in you." God said that you're valuable. You are so valuable that Almighty God, the Creator God, would identify with you 24/7. When Jesus said He would never leave you nor forsake you, He wasn't just using rhetoric. He dwells in you.

Look at the next passage:

> *And if the Spirit of him who raised Jesus from the dead is living in you, he who raised Christ from the dead will also give life to your mortal bodies through his Spirit, who lives in you.*
>
> ROMANS 8:11

Same idea, but this time Paul adds another idea. It's about the power of God. It says that the Spirit lives in you, but that's the same Spirit of God that raised Jesus from the dead. So unleashing the power of the Holy Spirit isn't something beyond you. If you're a Christ-follower, it's a recognition of how to cooperate with the Spirit of God that is within you.

II. JESUS' INSTRUCTION, RE: THE HOLY SPIRIT

Now Jesus gave us some very clear instructions, thank God. In Acts chapter 1, we're going to read three of four verses.

Let me just take a moment here. The New Testament

begins with four books: Matthew, Mark, Luke, and John—the Gospels. The Gospels tell us the story of Jesus' life from His birth through His resurrection, in essence from the vantage point of four different people. The next book in your New Testament—the book of Acts—tells us a different story. It's the story of Jesus' followers after Jesus returned to Heaven. In the first chapter of Acts, Jesus gives them their last instructions, and the rest of the book is an overview of the remaining time span of the New Testament. It's about a forty-year window. The New Testament by Old Testament standards, is a very short book. It deals with about a period of a hundred years. The Old Testament clearly deals with a much broader span of time. The children of Israel, for instance, were slaves in Egypt for four hundred years. The book of Judges is a period of time about four hundred years. Even though it's a short window of time, in the book of Acts we have this remarkable story—the Jesus-story—who, as the book of Acts opens, was last publicly seen dead on a Roman cross. And when the book of Acts concludes, the Jesus-story has made it all the way from Jerusalem to the streets of Rome and has even infiltrated Caesar's palace. It's an unimaginable story.

Jesus tells us the power that's going to make that happen in Acts

17

chapter 1 verse 4:

On one occasion, while he was eating with them, he gave them this command...

Circle that word "command." It's worth noting that it's not a suggestion, it's not a hint, it's not a prompt, it's not a nudge. Jesus gave them a commandment. Now I'm thinking if you watch someone die on a cross and be raised to life again and then He gives you a commandment, you might lean in a little bit, you think? Okay. Now here's the command:

Do not leave Jerusalem, but wait for the gift my Father promised, which you have heard me speak about. For John baptized with water, but in a few days you will be baptized with the Holy Spirit.

ACTS 1:4-5

What's the command? Don't leave Jerusalem until you're baptized with the Holy Spirit.

So when they met together, they asked him, "Lord, are you at this time going to restore the kingdom to Israel?" He said to them: "It is not for you to know the times or dates the Father has set by his own authority."

ACTS 1:6-7

The disciples aren't overly impressed with Jesus' dialogue. In fact, they have issues they want Him to address. They recognize now with clarity who He is and the power He represents, and they want to get their questions answered. They sound a lot like me. You know, I may take some time and read my Bible. I get done with my Bible reading, and then I whip out my to-do list and show it to God. Alright—*You know, God, I appreciate Your perspective, but have You looked at what I want You to do?* And that's a little bit of what the disciples are doing. Jesus gives them a commandment and they go, "Yeah, yeah, yeah, yeah, but are You...?" And Jesus, in an unrelenting fashion, brings them right back to center in verse 8. He says,

> *But you will receive power when the Holy Spirit comes on you; and you will be my witnesses in Jerusalem, and in all Judea and Samaria, and to the ends of the earth." After he said this, he was taken up before their very eyes, and a cloud hid him from their sight.*

ACTS 1:8-9

Now we all understand that last words have a heightened significance. In this case I would say emphatically so. Jesus' last words carry a unique authority, because of the way that He

19

exited—He simply ascended back to Heaven. He said, "You will be empowered to be my witnesses in Jerusalem and Judea and Samaria, to the ends of the earth when the Holy Spirit comes on you." And that is precisely what is described in the book of Acts—that story. Now I would submit to you it's nonsense for us to have an imagination that the purposes of God are going to go forth in our generation in some other way. Jesus is our teacher. He's the one that gave us the instructions. He gave us a commandment. He said, "Don't even begin your ministry." Now He was speaking to Matthew and James and John and Peter and Mary—the people that were closest to Him. He spent three years training them personally. They've walked with Him. They've traveled with Him. They were in the boat when He walked on the water. They were in the cemetery when Lazarus staggered out. They picked up baskets full of leftovers after they fed a multitude with a little boy's lunch. These folks have been up close and personal with Jesus; they've been able to ask Him privately about what He meant when He spoke publicly, and yet He said to them, "Don't you even begin your assignment until you are baptized with the Spirit." Now it seems to me if Jesus thought that was important for Matthew and Mark and James and Mary, that you and I perhaps should get in line. I'm just thinking.

III. THREE RESPONSES OF COOPERATION

Now Jesus actually talked to His disciples a great deal about the Holy Spirit; we have a lot of the narrative in Scripture. I'll give you some highlights.

In John's Gospel, Jesus said to His disciples, "It's better for you if I go away."

They struggled to believe that. They couldn't imagine anything was better than having Jesus with them. He was the most remarkable person they'd ever known.

He said, "It's better for you if I go away, because if I go away, the Father will send you a Comforter, a Counselor" (John 16:7, paraphrased). Jesus said to them, "The things I've been doing, you can do. And even greater things" (John 14:12, paraphrased). You know, it's the truth—the book of Acts describes that. Jesus ministered for three years publicly, and He had a reputation in Galilee and the northern part of Israel, and He was known to a lesser degree in Judea and the region surrounding Jerusalem. But His story was contained almost entirely in the Jewish villages in the land of Israel. Forty years after Jesus' ascension back to Heaven, the Jesus-story is known throughout the Roman world. It's a remarkable story—and it's not just a story—it's being demonstrated with signs and wonders and a demonstration of the power of God. It's precisely what Jesus said would happen. He said, "When the Holy Spirit comes upon you, you'll be empowered to be my witnesses in Jerusalem and Judea and Samaria to the uttermost parts of the earth."

Remember, the presence of the Spirit of God and the power of God are synonymous. You and I need the power of God. We've already identified those needs in our lives. The Holy Spirit is the key; we want to cooperate with Him. It seems to me in the clear narrative of Scripture that Spirit baptism is the doorway into experiencing a life filled with God's supernatural power. It's the way it's presented to us in the book of Acts. It's never withdrawn; it's never canceled. The order of the commandment hasn't been somehow wiped away. It's important. Now the challenge becomes how we cooperate with the Holy Spirit.

Now I want to give you three simple ideas for cooperating with the Person of the Holy Spirit. I have observed a behavior amongst those of us who are Christ-followers. Now I've been a Christ-follower a long time, and we tend to pursue our faith as if we're earning merit badges or gathering diplomas or awards of some sort, and we tell our God stories in that fashion. It's not uncommon to say, "Yes, I'm a Christ-follower. I made a profession of faith in 1822. I remember right where I was. You know, it was Brother John Birch and I got a certificate and it's right there on the wall. See? 'Christ-follower.' And then I got baptized. I got dunked. It was in the creek. It was Cedar Creek on Sunday. And I got another certificate and I put that on the wall. See? 'Baptized.' My name's on it. And maybe you say, "You know, and I've received Spirit baptism and I've done that and I've got that on the wall." And then we point and say, "That's my journey."

I would submit to you that those experiences with the Lord are simply invitations into a life. They don't define your journey; they simply say you've got the privilege now of growing up in the Lord. See, the goal of being a Christ-follower isn't being birthed into the Kingdom and then getting your rattle and your paci and waiting for the trumpet to blow. You don't want to show up before Saint Peter at the Pearly Gates with pampers on. "Woo, I made it!" It will be awkward. We want to grow up in the Lord, and in the same way, we want to learn to cooperate with the Spirit of God.

That's what the story's about in the book of Acts. Peter and James and John—they struggled mightily to understand what was happening with Jesus. Time and time again it says they were confused, that they didn't understand. Jesus said, "Are you so dull?" They were! But after the second chapter, when the Holy Spirit was poured out, it says that they began to pray in a language that they didn't understand and give glory to God. A crowd gathers and Peter preaches, and thousands of people in Jerusalem acknowledge Jesus of Nazareth as the Messiah and are willing to be baptized in public. Just a few weeks earlier, the streets of that same city were filled with thousands of people saying of Jesus, "Crucify him!" And Peter was hiding. Now he's standing before the crowd saying, "The one you crucified, God made Messiah." And they respond. Thousands of them baptized. The whole city is stirred and shaken. What's the difference? The presence of the Holy Spirit in their lives in a new way.

If Jesus' ministry didn't begin until the descent of the Spirit, and the disciples' ministry changed dramatically after the outpouring of the Holy Spirit, I would submit to you it's nonsense for you and me to think we're going to out-study evil—that we're going to out-organize ungodliness. We need the help of the Holy Spirit because in His presence is the power of Almighty God.

A. PRAYER

So how do we cooperate with Him? I just want to suggest three very simple ideas. None of them will be new to you, but the implementation of them often remains distant in our lives. The first one is about prayer. Decide to become a person who prays. Now I know the challenge this is, but we want to at least acknowledge that we want to be students of prayer. But I want to encourage you if you're in the habit of saying, "I don't pray," to stop that. Because in essence when you say, "I don't pray," what you're saying is, "I'm not interested in the power of God." And I don't typically think that's what you mean. It would be more helpful to say, "I'm not comfortable praying," or "I'm not comfortable speaking out loud," or "I'm not comfortable speaking in front of other people," or "I'm a little reluctant to talk about my faith." All of those statements may be accurate descriptions, but when you say, "I don't pray," you say, "I don't care about the power of God." I don't believe that to be true for most of us.

Look in 1 Corinthians 14. Paul is writing to the church at Corinth, and he said,

> *I thank God, I speak in tongues more than all of you;*
>
> 1 CORINTHIANS 14:18

The events of Acts chapter 2 and the day of Pentecost were not limited to a singular day in history. In fact in Acts 2:38-39, Peter said to the inhabitants of Jerusalem, "the gift" of that day was "for you and for your children and for your children's children and for all who are far off." I think we have to open our hearts to the Person of the Holy Spirit in any way we know how to cooperate with Him.

Look at Romans 8: 26. It says,

> *In the same way, the Spirit helps us in our weakness.*
>
> ROMANS 8:26

Let's pause there just a moment. I love that phrase.

It says that the Spirit—it's a capital "S"; it's the Holy Spirit—helps us in our weaknesses. Now this is counter-intuitive because of the way we learn to pursue God in organized ways. It's not evil, but to come to church we clean up and we spray up and we sit up, right? And you file into the sanctuary and you sit and you look forward and you look at the person next to you and you kind of calmly go, *Bless you*, and the notion is that's how we are 24/7. Not. It's not hard to hustle the preacher. He's not that clever. But we don't con God. God, the Bible says, knows the thoughts and intents of our heart. The fear is that if the people that you worship with knew who you really were, they wouldn't worship with you. Please hear what the scripture says: "The Holy Spirit helps us in our weaknesses." He knows our shortcomings and our frailties, our greatest fears. He knows everything about us, and He helps us. He doesn't condemn us. He doesn't demean us. Your adversaries will exploit your weaknesses. Your adversaries celebrate your weakness. Your adversaries will remind you of your weakness. The Holy Spirit helps us in our weaknesses. I want to get to know Him. He will help me where I am weak. That is such a powerful statement. And then this passage unpacks that for us a little bit.

How does He help us in our weaknesses?

We do not know what we ought to pray for...

Isn't that the truth? I mean, we may know what we want, but we don't really know what we ought to pray for. I'm so conscious of that in my own life. I mean, I have things that I'm disquieted about, or there are places I want God's help, but I don't really know what I ought to pray for. It says He will help.

But the Spirit himself intercedes for us with groans that words cannot express. And he who searches our hearts knows the mind of the Spirit, because the Spirit intercedes for the saints in accordance with God's will.

ROMANS 8:26-27

What a marvelous promise—that the Holy Spirit will intercede—will pray through you beyond what you're consciously able to shape words for. Thank God.

That's such a powerful part of my relationship with my congregation. Years ago when the church was much, much smaller, I developed a habit of cleaning the sanctuary. I would be in the sanctuary, and I would walk through the room when it was empty. We only had a about six rows of chairs for our one service, but I would walk through the rows of the chairs

27

and I would touch each chair and pray for the people, because there weren't but a few handfuls of us there. I knew everybody that came, and they all sat in the same spot. It's your chair after all. Right? We all know church world. I developed a habit of walking through the room and praying for the people, and the habit persists until today. Now the dynamics are different. I don't know every seat that everybody sits in or every person by name any longer, but you know, back in the day my prayers were inadequate. If I had known I was absolutely hardwired into God and a person I was praying for would receive the first three things I asked for, I would have messed it up. I would have prayed that they got a new washer and dryer, and they wanted a new microwave. God would have answered my three prayers and they would have been delivered to their house and they'd want to know who messed up because they didn't need the stuff that I'd gotten an answer to prayer for. And I learned to invite the Holy Spirit to help me pray for the people that God had sent me to serve. I didn't understand back in the day that He was training me for today. It's such a freedom for me to know that I can pray for you—that God knows what you need—that He knows the details, and He knows the circumstances.

You see, we unleash the power of God when we present ourselves to pray. When we say, "I'm too busy to pray," or "I'm not interested in prayer," or "I don't know how to pray." What you're saying is: "I have no intention of cooperating with the power of God." Don't say that. Say, "I'd like to learn. I'll make some time for that." In fact, I'll make one suggestion that will dramatically change your prayer life if you'll consider it. It's not rocket science, folks, or I wouldn't have it. Make an appointment with yourself for a time of prayer. Now I'm not talking about a three-hour block of time or saying you have to sit in a yoga position and hum. You may start with a five-minute block of time. Put it on your calendar like you do an appointment with anyone else and say, "On these days, I'm going to take that block of time and make an appointment. I'm going to pray." Maybe you read a scripture and then you take a minute or two, and you do some journaling. You can do that. You could take a chapter from the book of Psalms. You can do it a lot of ways. You may just sit quietly before the Lord, but make an appointment with the Lord to pray.

That's not how most of us learn to pray. Most of us learn to pray in the moment, right? During commercials, at halftime, or when we're driving and our cell phone's dead. I can't talk to anybody else so, *Hey God.* We kind of have this spontaneous notion that Almighty God—the Creator of Heaven and the Earth, the One who can part the ocean or raise you to life again, who holds your eternity in His hands, the Judge of all living things—should respond to me in the whim of a moment. And in His mercy and His grace sometimes He does.

But I would submit to you an appointment for prayer suggests all the other things that you know an appointment suggests, that you attach value enough to meeting that person that you'll schedule it—that you have the humility to say, "I would like your attention for a moment please, and I will present myself at the appointed time." See, it seems nonsensical to me to imagine that you really attach great value to God and you're not even willing to put Him into your plan. Now, I don't want to limit your prayer to that. I understand that the Bible says to pray without ceasing and that we're to live our lives 24/7 with an awareness of God. I don't want to limit you to a five-minute prayer block. But I do want to plant a seed that attaching enough value to warrant scheduling the appointment will change the story in your heart.

Learning new things is often awkward or uncomfortable. Do not stop praying because it feels awkward. As you persist you will gain confidence, become more aware of the Lord, and less self-conscious.

B. EXPECTANCY

Alright, prayer is one component of cooperation. The second one is expectancy. I've spent my life around Church and Christ-followers and God's people, and it seems to me we have a pretty low threshold of expectation. We don't really have a high degree of expectancy that God will do anything. In fact, we're usually surprised, and it's unfortunate.

One of the things I find when I read the book of Acts and the rest of the New Testament is the people that knew Jesus came away from that season with Him with an expectation that God would move. We have to cultivate that expectation. It's a choice we make initially.

I want to give you one example from Scripture. It's when Mary and Joseph bring infant Jesus to the Temple to be circumcised on His eighth day. It's according to the Law of Moses, and when they bring Him to the Temple there are a couple of people in the Temple who recognize this infant Jesus as the Messiah. One of them is an elderly woman—her name is Anna—she's a prophetess, and when she sees the baby Jesus, she speaks to Mary and Joseph and to the people who are there.

At that very moment she came up and began giving thanks to God, and continued to speak of Him to all those who were looking for the redemption of Jerusalem.

LUKE 2:38 (NASB®)

Now they're in a public place. There are hundreds of people no doubt gathered there, and it says when Anna began to speak to Mary and Joseph regarding the new born child, she didn't speak to them alone, she spoke to a subset of the people who were gathered.

Did you catch how they were defined? She spoke to those who

were "looking for the redemption of Jerusalem." Not everybody in the Temple was looking for the Messiah. Some of them were there because it was the place to be. It was the day when they brought newborns. There were no doubt dozens of families presenting. There were all sorts of people milling about. There were priests and Temple workers—a whole collection of people, but there was a group of people there that were expecting the Messiah and Anna spoke to them.

Expect a miracle! Something good is going to happen to you!

I want to be included in the group of people who are not just attending the services or are caught in religious activities. I want to be included in the group of people that are expecting God to do something. It's important. We're not just the collectors of Bible trivia. We are not just a people that are caught under the responsibility of religious behavior. We are the people of Almighty God in the earth, and we expect Him to move in our generation as He has in every generation through the lives of men and women of faith. We want to cooperate with His Spirit. We want to welcome Him into our lives. My Bible says that Jesus Christ is the same yesterday, today, and forever; He doesn't change. And we want to open our hearts and our imaginations to the expectation that God will work.

You say, "Well I don't understand that. You say that, but I still have problems." Me too. And the people in the Bible certainly did as well. We've carried a mistaken idea that it's enough to say you believe in God and that you believe God does miracles and that you believe in the power of God. To believe that does not mean you never have problems and stresses and disappointments and heartaches. Because every miracle story you know in the Bible is in response to a hard place.

It's important to remember that before Daniel was delivered from the lion's den, Daniel had to go check the lion's teeth. And before he got to the lion's den he was betrayed by people who had wrong motives. Daniel had the well-being of the empire at heart and they were jealous of him so they orchestrated a set of circumstances that had him condemned to death. The whole scenario is unfair and unfortunate.

Every Bible story you know is a response to pain and heartache and difficulty. Even Jesus' resurrection is a response to an unfair execution. So saying that you believe in the power of God is not denying the challenges of your life. It's simply extending to you a resource beyond yourself. We are, after all, the people of God, and we believe He's involved in our lives. We want to create in our heart the expectation that God will move.

"Well, why hasn't He moved before?" I don't know; I'm not God. Sometimes I read those stories and I think, *God, why, why did You do it that way?* And you know what He says? "It's none of your business." If He'd wanted me to know, He would've told me. It's not the way I would have done it on so many occasions.

A woman who has had an issue of hemorrhaging for many years; she lost everything that she has. She spent it, and she's not better before she gets to Jesus. I'm thinking, *Wow—Lazarus—why'd the dude have to die and have a funeral and be buried and everybody sit around and cry for days.* Jesus did that on purpose. You say, "Well it worked out in the end." Well, it may have, but give me the choice between being dead for three days or just being healed, and I'm going with the healing every time.

So don't let the difficulties of your life rob you of your expectation that God will move. Get out of the seat of the skeptic. It's not a fruitful place to stay. We all sit there for a little while, but let it be musical chairs. Get up and find a better seat.

Skepticism is not a sign of intellectual prowess. Often, skepticism indicates my own tendency to be a rebel. It is more profitable to cooperate with God.

C. HONOR GOD'S WORD

Now, there's one more piece I'll give you. Prayer, expectancy, and honoring God's Word. Cultivate the habit of honoring the

Word of God in your life. Treat God like He's smarter than you. Don't read God's Word to decide what you disagree with; let God's Word read you to decide what God disagrees with in you.

Now, I've mentioned Luke 2; I want to step back into that narrative because you know the scenario by now. Mary and Joseph with baby Jesus are in the Temple. The first man they meet that recognizes Jesus is a man named Simeon. Let's read it. It's Luke 2:25:

> *Now there was a man in Jerusalem called Simeon, who was righteous and devout. He was waiting for the consolation of Israel, and the Holy Spirit was upon him. It had been revealed to him by the Holy Spirit that he would not die before he had seen the Lord's Christ. Moved by the Spirit, he went into the temple courts. When the parents brought in the child Jesus to do for him what the custom of the Law required, Simeon took him in his arms and praised God, saying: "Sovereign Lord, as you have promised, you may now dismiss your servant in peace. For my eyes have seen your salvation, which you have prepared in the sight of all nations: a light for revelation to the Gentiles, and the glory of your people Israel."*

LUKE 2:25-32

Let's look at those first few verses about Simeon. In each verse there's a phrase repeated. Something was accomplished in his life by the presence of the Holy Spirit, and Luke uses the literary devise of repetition to draw our attention to the Person of the Holy Spirit in Simeon's life. Look back with me a moment. In verse twenty-five it says of Simeon, "The Holy Spirit was upon him." In verse twenty-six it says something had been revealed to him by the Holy Spirit, that he would see the Messiah before he died. How did he know that? It was revealed to him by the Holy Spirit. In the next verse, in verse twenty-seven, it says he went into the Temple court that day moved by the Holy Spirit— prompted by the Holy Spirit.

Luke is emphasizing that what's happening in Simeon's life is a result of the Person of the Holy Spirit's involvement with him. If he wasn't trying to emphasize that, you could have made that statement in a far more efficient way. There was a godly man named Simeon that recognized Jesus in the Temple. But Luke is recognizing something for us. Who's the author of the book of Acts? It's not a trick. Luke. This is in the Gospel of Luke, but Luke's thought and Luke's objective in writing is consistent. There was an emphasis upon the Person of the Holy Spirit, because again, in Luke's language and in Luke's thought, the Person of the Holy Spirit and the power of God are synonymous. Now watch what happens in Simeon's life. It says that he's moved by the Spirit, and he went into the Temple courts. I love that statement. Simeon has had a revelation by the Spirit of God that he's going to see the Messiah before he dies. And where do we find Simeon on this day? He's in the Temple. He's in the Temple on the day when they're presenting the babies for circumcision. The Temple Mount, Herod's Temple Mount, is an enormous place. All sorts of gathering areas and different things happening, and Simeon is standing there where the newborn children are being presented in the Temple. Now there are many places in the land of Israel where you could have presented your child, but the Temple in Jerusalem is the epitome of all the places to go. It is the expression of the religious authority of the nation, and so it's a logical place to look, of all the places Simeon could have been. Did you know in Jerusalem in the first century there was a hippodrome, a place for horse races? He could have been at the trifecta window between the second and third race. There was a Roman theater in first century Jerusalem. He could have been at the theater seeing the latest presentation. Neither of the above options was evil or wicked, but there had been something revealed to him, so what does Simeon do with his time and his days? He spends time in the place where the baby would most likely be presented. It's the most likely opportunity for him to see the child.

Unleashing the power of the Holy Spirit in your life and mine has a great deal to do with the desire to see God move. If you don't care about that, if you're not interested in Him, you can relax. It's highly improbable He will bother you. God does not intrude where He's not invited. But if you have a desire, a hunger—the Bible says that if we hunger and thirst after righteousness, that we'll be filled. In Hebrews it says that God is the rewarder of those who diligently seek Him. We need His help. When you need the help from a physician, you'll make an appointment, you'll drive to their offices, you'll go for testing. If they recommend you go to another hospital, you'll go to that hospital. If they send you to another city, if it's a serious enough diagnosis, you'll go to that city. You'll endure treatment protocols that are difficult and life threatening because you need the outcome.

When it comes to the things of the Lord, we should have at least as much perseverance as we have in the medical community. We've been pretty casual. Honestly, I think we've been disrespectful. Almighty God—Creator God—deserves our best.

Going back to Simeon, I don't believe the words he spoke were some unique creation of the Holy Spirit. I gave you three passages from Isaiah:

The people who walk in darkness will see a great light; those who live in a dark land, the light will shine on them.

ISAIAH 9:2 (NASB®)

I will also make You a light of the nations so that My salvation may reach to the end of the earth.

ISAIAH 49:6 (NASB®)

Pay attention to Me, O My people, and give ear to Me, O My nation; For a law will go forth from Me, and I will set My justice for a light of the peoples.

ISAIAH 51:4 (NASB®)

What Simeon is doing is reciting the idea that the prophets had given him about the Messiah. He had spent enough time in the Word—God's Word—he knew the prophets well enough that when he had the revelation of who the child was, he knew what that child was going to do.

My invitation to you is to spend enough time with the Word of God so that God's character can begin to emerge in your heart. Be aware of what God is going to do so that when He reveals to you a God-moment, you know His perspective on that place. It's very difficult to argue you care about God if you've never read the Book. I don't say that to condemn you or to shame you or put another burden on you. I'm not trying to add to your to-do list. I want to learn how to unleash the power of the Spirit of God, and it isn't arbitrary. God's not capricious. You can choose a path that will lead you to the Lord. What an honor. What a privilege.

And it can start with the simplest of prayers—something like this in your heart, *Holy Spirit, You're welcome in my life. I want to welcome You in my life. I want to cooperate with You.*

Let that little prayer begin to resonate in your heart. It will change everything.

PRAYER: Heavenly Father, pour out Your Spirit upon my life. I offer myself as a living sacrifice, yielded to You. I want to know You in the power of Your truth. I choose the truth for my life, turning away from all deception. May the words of my mouth and the meditations of my heart be pleasing in Your sight, in Jesus' name. Amen.

UNLEASHING THE POWER OF THE HOLY SPIRIT

THE DESERT PLACES

There's a lot of confusion, a lot of anxiety, maybe even a lot of fear in Christendom around the topic of the Holy Spirit. With God's help, I would like to help diminish that in your life.

The premise so far, and our foundation moving forward is this: From the first chapter of the Bible in Genesis until the conclusion of the story in Revelation—the power of God and the presence of the Holy Spirit are almost synonymous.

Now why that's relevant to you and me is we're trusting God for breakthroughs in our lives. Whether it's physically or emotionally or financially or relationally, we're saying, *God, we need Your power to help us.* So if you've accepted the notion that the power of God and the Person of the Holy Spirit go together, asking God for His power but being reluctant to cooperate with the Holy Spirit is irrational.

We come from many different backgrounds, and we've learned different things in different ways about the Person of the Holy

Spirit. My suggestion is simply this—let a prayer begin in your heart that says, *Holy Spirit You're welcome in my life.* Then put your hand over your mouth. Don't put qualifications, don't put limits, don't say what you will do or you won't do or how He has to present Himself.

I can tell you this about the Person of the Holy Spirit: He will never embarrass you, nor will He violate your will. He won't make you do something you don't want to do. I've had people come to me and say, "You know, I didn't want to do it, but the Lord made me." No, He didn't. You know occasionally someone will approach me and say, "Pastor, I don't want to say this to you, but the Lord's making me." No, He's not. I'll save you that awkward moment. God doesn't do that. He doesn't violate our free will.

In fact, I'll help you. You can distinguish between the Holy Spirit and an unholy, demonic spirit. A demonic spirit will bully and intimidate you—it will violate your own sense. People will say, "I didn't want to do it, but I couldn't stop." That's unholy. So don't be afraid of the Holy Spirit.

I'll tell you something else about Him. He won't come where He's not welcome. If you don't have a desire for His presence in your life and His involvement in your life, He won't bother you. So you need not be concerned about that. He only comes where He's welcome—where He's invited—where there's desire to honor Jesus.

In fact, if you want to facilitate His presence, cultivate in yourself a desire to honor Jesus. I've made that a point in my life for the last several years. If I'm showing up someplace, I want folks to know I'm coming as a Jesus-advocate. And the reason I've tried to be consistent with that is I want a consistent presence of the Spirit of God in my life.

I. INTO THE DESERT

Building on the same theme, I want to explore with you biblically this notion of "desert places".

I have come to truly enjoy the desert. For me, that's been predominantly in the nation of Israel. I haven't been in the southwestern part of the United States a great deal or other deserts of the world, but I've spent a good deal of time in the deserts of Israel. For me it's a place that used to be very unwelcoming and harsh and hostile—really to be avoided in favor of air conditioned places with lots of water. But now I have come to truly enjoy it.

There's a biblical place assigned to the desert that is very, very unique. So I want to use that biblical narrative and also an image that it suggests to us. There are not only physical deserts, sometimes there are desert seasons of our lives. Have you noticed?

They're dry places—barren places. And if you're walking through one of those desert seasons—a dry season or a barren season or a time of minimal resources—I want you to know this, and I hope we'll see it so clearly from Scripture, that in those desert places the Spirit of God is with you. In fact, I can say it more directly—oftentimes the Spirit of God led you there. He took you there.

Now, God is not a child abuser. He doesn't break your legs to teach you a lesson. But sometimes He leads us to places where we can be better students.

I've learned something from being in the desert places physically. You can't fight the desert. It doesn't work well. You can't outwork the desert. The desert is a place that you have to learn to cooperate with your environment. You have to recognize the limits that are there and work within those limits. It's true physically, and I would submit to you it's true in those spiritual places as well.

In the desert you drink when you're not thirsty. If you wait until you're thirsty, it's too late—you're already behind the hydration curve. In the desert you rest before you're exhausted, because the elements are too harsh and the demands on you physically are too great. If you get exhausted, it's very difficult to recover. In the desert you listen when there's not a great deal of noise because usually the messages in the desert come to you in a much gentler way. It's not a place of a great deal of noise and audio clutter, so you have to listen for the more subtle things. It's a good place.

In fact, biblically there are some things that happen in the desert uniquely, and I made you a list. It's not intended to be a complete list by any means, but rather something of a sampling. I just want to plant the seed in your heart that the desert, both physically and spiritually, can be a good place.

In Scripture it's a useful place. There it's a place of renewal, revelation, deliverance, provision, refuge, and preparation.

All of those things God did for His people in desert places, both physically and spiritually. If you're in one of those seasons, God has not abandoned you, He hasn't overlooked you, He hasn't forgotten you. It isn't that He's ignoring you.

I would submit to you He's given you a season for a tremendous engagement in your life.

II. MOSES AND HEBREW PEOPLE

Let's start with one of the more familiar desert journeys. It's Moses and the Hebrew people. Now you know a good deal about Moses. Hollywood has helped with that. He grows up as a prince of Egypt, and in an act of violence he murders an Egyptian and he flees Egypt. He happens to end up in the backside of the desert where he stays for a long time. He has a God-encounter at a burning bush, and God gives him a new assignment. He sends him back to Egypt, and Moses is most reluctant to go.

In fact, he tries every excuse he can think of until God gets angry with him. But he eventually cooperates with the purposes of God.

Isn't it good to know that some of the greatest men and women of faith weren't excited about God's plan for them? That helps me. You ever get a sense God's inviting you to do something and you go, "Ohhh, send Pastor." Right? "Not my job. That's what we pay him for." You're not unique. I've been reluctant oftentimes when I've sensed God pushing His initiative, or I had an awareness that perhaps there was an invitation from Him.

Don't let that first "no" that comes out of you be your final answer. Phone a friend. Get a lifeline. Do something.

Do not be afraid of God's plan or His invitations. He loves you. He is wiser than you are. He knows the end at the beginning. Trust Him—you will not regret it. God's invitations may stir an inner struggle. Choose Him anyway!

Moses returns to Egypt and one of the great confrontations in all of history took place between the spokesperson for the slaves—the Hebrew slaves—and the Pharaoh of Egypt. Pharaoh said "No," and God said "Yes." And for the first several plagues the magicians of Egypt duplicated God's supernatural involvement.

Satan is an impostor. Jesus said he's the father of all lies. And to the best extent of his ability—his abilities are limited; He's not infinite like our God is—he will duplicate what Almighty God does. That's the reason the end of the ages will be concluded with a false Christ—an antichrist—accompanied by a false prophet. The Antichrist will be a religious person. There'll be miracles and the supernatural, because the power behind them is the imitator of the true God.

The magicians of Egypt duplicated the first few plagues and Pharaoh's heart, it says, was hardened. Until finally the last of the plagues was the Passover. The Spirit of Death passed through the land of Egypt, and the first born in the land died in every household except in the places where the blood of the lamb was on the door post.

And when the sun came up, the Egyptians drove the Hebrews out of their nation. They gave them their gold and their silver. They said, "Leave. We don't want you. We don't want the sun to go down another night with you here. We're afraid." And God led the Hebrew people after hundreds of years of slavery into freedom.

Do you know why they were slaves? It wasn't racial. The Bible tells us that they prospered so much, that the Hebrew people were so blessed by God, that their lives became so abundant, the Egyptians were jealous of them and said, "If we don't do something about this, they will rule over us." So they made them slaves. They had a numerical advantage, and they were jealous of their prosperity.

Did you know God wants to bless you? Christians are weird on this point. I'm not exactly sure why. I have a few theories, but we get real tense. They'll say, "You're not one of those 'prosperity people,' are you?" And I'll say, "Yeah! What are you, one of those poverty people? If you are, just start mailing me your paycheck. Don't be half blessed, take a double portion."

Now you can't evaluate your spirituality by your bank balance. That's nonsense. It's foolish to suggest the car you drive or the label in your clothing makes you holier or less. Nonsense. But the Bible's very clear—God desires to bless His people, and abundance is a gift from Him.

I'll tell you the truth. I think one reason we don't want to open that whole discussion is we don't want to invite a God-discussion about our resources. We want to act like that's ours.

I understand that, but what you should understand is that notion is a reflection of the tremendous affluence that we live in. We are so blessed and we have so much that you have the notion that you can get along financially without God. Folks, it's not true.

With what's ahead of us, the only stability and the only security and the only certainty is understanding that God is our source.

What I want to call your attention to is the way God led them.

By day the LORD went ahead of them in a pillar of cloud to guide them on their way and by night in a pillar of fire to give them light, so that they could travel by day or night. Neither the pillar of cloud by day nor the pillar of fire by night left its place in front of the people.

EXODUS 13:21-22

God provided a physical, visible, tangible beacon to lead the people. By day a cloud to provide shade, at night a fire to provide comfort. He physically made evident to them the path He wanted them to walk. He programmed their GPS. He said, "This is the way to go."

Remember, they've been slaves. They have been slaves in Egypt longer than the United States has been a nation. There's a big group of people released, and God physically engineers their pathway. There's more than one way to get to the Promised Land—the land that He's told them about. When He brought them out of Egyptian slavery, it was for the purpose of bringing them into a land that flowed with milk and honey.

When God delivers you out of a place, it's because He intends to bring you to a better place. So understand, when you're asking for a breakthrough, when you're asking for God's deliverance, He's going to bring you to a new place and you can't grow without changing.

They could have gone along the coastal highway. There literally was a highway along the coast. It was flatter ground, it was easier to travel, and there were some cities along the way. There would have been food and water and an easier, shorter, more direct path to their destination. But God led them with His pillar of cloud and pillar of fire into the desert—no Walmart, no Mickey D's.

Scholars argue a little bit about how many people were released from Egyptian slavery. The lowest numbers are usually over two hundred thousand. The highest numbers exceed a million people. Either way, that's a lot of folks, and God led all of them into the wilderness.

Now it doesn't stop there. Look at Exodus 15. It says, "Moses led Israel from the Red Sea…" The Red Sea is where they had this tremendous victory. The Egyptian army drowned.

Oh, by the way, God led them to a beach. You know, their first camping spot was on the beach. Wasn't that good of God? Now the down side of that was their enemies changed their mind and chased them, so they were pinned between the beach and their enemy's army.

They're out-manned, they're out-gunned, they're under-trained, they're under-resourced. And God said, "No matter. Watch this. Moses, stretch that rod out over the water." The waters part, and the Egyptian army drowns after the Hebrews have escaped.

They had their first celebration—an all-out celebration. It says the women danced on the shores of the Red Sea and sang, "God has thrown the horse and rider into the water."

Now this is the very same chapter—that's Exodus 15 in the same chapter. It says,

> *Moses led Israel from the Red Sea and they went into the Desert of Shur. For three days they traveled in the desert without finding water. When they came to Marah, they could not drink its water because it was bitter. So the people grumbled against Moses, saying, "What are we to drink?"*

EXODUS 15:22-24

Marah is a transliteration. It means they took the Hebrew letters and chose the English equivalent and just gave you the English spelling of the Hebrew word. The Hebrew word *Marah* means "bitter."

The whole nation grumbled; Moses prayed. God showed him a piece of wood and said, "If you'll throw the wood in the water, it will become drinkable."

God parted the ocean, decimated Egypt, drowned the Egyptian army, then led the people not only into the desert, but to a place where they couldn't drink the water. They're not there by accident. They didn't take a wrong turn. God led them there.

Do you have room in your imagination for this? He led them to a place that didn't fully meet their need, and some grumbled—most grumbled—and Moses prayed.

In Hebrew the word for *wood* could also designate a "growing tree." It could designate a cross. It's a type, a pattern, of the cross of Jesus. Moses put the wood in the water, and they could drink it.

And after the people had their fill, God said to them, "I'm the Lord, your God, that delivered you from Egypt, and I will be Jehovah Rapha to you." *Rapha* is the Modern Hebrew word for "physician." He said, "I'll be the Lord, your Doctor, and I will not put on you any of the diseases that you saw on the Egyptians, if you will obey Me."

God took them to a place where they would have to listen—in

the desert—and He said, "While I have your attention, I'll be your doctor. You won't be sick like you saw the Egyptians were if you'll just cooperate with Me." God led them to that place.

Do you believe God would lead you to a desert place so you could get to know Him better? See, it's a recalibration of our imagination of what it means to be a Christ-follower. I think we tend to imagine the power of God is some supernatural force to help us get our way. Right? I mean, we may not say it out loud, but that's really kind of what's in our heart. *God, how can I get You to give me an advantage in business? How can I help you to give me an upper hand in the places in my life where there seems to be tension?*

And I think what God is really interested in is our desire for His way and His will in our lives. The real challenge we have is a lot of times that's just not so important to us. Do you know why? We are a race of rebels.

In the beginning of the story, God created a garden, the most beautiful place our world has ever known, and then He created a man and a woman and put them in the midst of the garden and He said, "It is all yours. It is all yours. I give you authority over it all. Take dominion over the whole thing." He said, "Now there's that one tree—don't eat out of that tree." So what'd they do? They rebelled.

See, the story of this Book—it isn't complex. It's about how we are a race of rebels. The people that He led out of Egypt after hundreds of years of slavery—He protected them in every way. What is the story of that Exodus generation? How would you describe them in a word? They were rebels—over and over and over again, until finally they got to the shores of the Promise Land. They saw it, and they said, "We don't want to do that. We don't want to do that. We know it's there and yes, it's a land that flows with milk and honey and the produce of the land is amazing, but we don't want to do that."

Then it said that God got angry with them, and He said, "Alright, I will feed you. I'll take care of you. I will watch over you. I'll protect you from your enemies until your days under the sun are spent, but you'll die in this desert."

I would encourage you today not to be a rebel. There's not a great future in being a rebel. "Humble yourself," the Bible says, "under the mighty hand of God." He'll bring good things to you. Being a Christ-follower is not loathsome, it's not burdensome, it will not diminish your life.

And if you're walking through a season in that desert place, God hasn't abandoned you. He has something good for you—He wants to bring you into a broader place, a wider place, a new place.

Let me highlight another passage. It's Nehemiah chapter 9. Nehemiah is in exile. Jerusalem's been destroyed. He's living in a foreign land. He's the cup-bearer to the Persian King—modern day Iran—and he hears that Jerusalem has been destroyed and he accepts a God assignment to go back to leave his life of comfort and ease and go to the desert and rebuild the wall around the city. It's a big task.

He's an organized person; he gets together everything he needs. And when he gets back he finds that his adversaries are more persistent, that the task is greater than he imagined, and the strength of his co-workers is diminished.

And the story he reaches for to find security for himself and his team is the story of the Exodus. It's their family story. It's our family story. The God that parted the Red Sea is the God that watches over my life. The God that brought manna in the desert is the God that's watching over my resource stream.

Nehemiah understood that, and he used it for his own life. You're not being presumptive or arrogant or diminished or naïve or anything else when you accept the Word of God and believe it will dictate the terms of your life.

Listen to what Nehemiah says:

> *Because of your great compassion you did not abandon them in the desert. By day the pillar of cloud did not cease to guide them on their path, nor the pillar of fire by night to shine on the way they were to take. You gave your good Spirit to instruct them.*

NEHEMIAH 9:19-20

Our theme is Unleashing the Power of the Holy Spirit. Whom did Nehemiah recognize was the force that guided the people and instructed them? Think of what came out of that season in the desert: They got the Ten Commandments, God gave them a form of worship, He gave them the orders for the Tabernacle, He gave them the orders for the priesthood.

You know why that was important? For four hundred years they've lived in Egypt. You think they were a little influenced by Egyptian culture? The Egyptians worshipped gods that had the heads of animals and the bodies of humans. They knew Egyptian holidays. They knew Egyptian customs. They knew Egyptian food. They knew Egyptian health practices. They were a group of people highly influenced by a pagan culture and God says, "Let me help you learn how to worship me—I'm a Holy God. Moses, come up the mountain, and nobody touch him while he's up there."

And Nehemiah, hundreds of years later says, "God sent His good Spirit to instruct them." That same good Spirit is here to help you and me. Don't be afraid of Him. Don't limit Him. We want to be in the world but not of the world, and the power of God present to help us with that transition is the power of the Holy Spirit.

If you want your children to be godly and pure and clean before God, help them build a relationship with the Holy Spirit.

———

You did not withhold your manna from their mouths, and you gave them water for their thirst. For forty years you sustained them in the desert; they lacked nothing, their clothes did not wear out nor did their feet become swollen.

NEHEMIAH 9:20-21

You ought to circle those three words in your Bible—"they lacked nothing." They didn't lack anything. For forty years God took care of them—not for a day, not on a weekend retreat, not over the holiday—for forty years God provided for the every need of a lot of people.

———

I included that whole passage for that last phrase. Every time I read it, it makes me smile.

It says that their feet didn't swell... Huh?

I've been in that Negev Desert. It is a brutal, brutal place. The temperature routinely climbs above a hundred and ten. It's not a sandy desert like we saw in *Lawrence of Arabia*. It's a rocky desert. The footing is uneven. It has hills and valleys and canyons you've got to climb—nothing's level. There is no shade. God said, "I provided everything they needed." And the punch line, the exclamation point is even their feet didn't swell.

Folks, if we went into that desert this morning, you'd swell up. I was there as a young buck and my feet swelled. It makes me smile. God says, "I even watched over their fluid balance."

He cares for us. He does. He led them into that place and He said, "I fed them, I gave them water, their clothes were okay, even their feet didn't swell. I led them there."

You can trust Him. *Holy Spirit, help me learn to cooperate with You. You're for my good. You're not opposed to me.*

If you imagine Him to be opposed to you—it's highly probable you're standing in a rebellious place. Don't stay there.

III. JESUS

Somebody will say to me, "Well, Pastor, that's really good, but that's Old Testament and I'm a New Testament kind of person."

Well, let's look at Jesus for a minute. In the Gospel of Luke, it says,

> *Jesus, full of the Holy Spirit, returned from the Jordan and was led around by the Spirit in the wilderness for forty days...*
>
> LUKE 4:1-2 (NASB®)

The Jordan River—He'd gone for baptism. It's where the Holy Spirit descended on Him, you remember that? It says after His baptism He was led by the Spirit—not led by evil—led by the Spirit into the wilderness.

Wilderness here is a term meaning it wasn't in an urban area. It wasn't a populated area and the non-urban, non-populated areas of Israel are the desert. He was led by the Spirit of God into the desert where for forty days He was tempted by the Devil. The Holy Spirit led Him to a place where He was tempted by the Devil.

> *He ate nothing during those days, and when they had ended,*
> *He became hungry.*
>
> LUKE 4:2 (NASB®)

No kidding. Forty days.

> *And the devil said to Him, "If You are the Son of God, tell this*
> *stone to become bread"*
>
> LUKE 4:3 (NASB®)

If you want to get to the character of the Devil, just drop the "d." He's evil. He approaches Jesus at the point of great vulnerability, and he'll do the same to you and to me.

He said, "If you're the Son of God, and if you happen to be

hungry after forty days, you can make bread out of rocks—IF You're the Son of God."

He knew very well who He was or he wouldn't have been tempting Him. He wanted Jesus to rebel. He's an impostor. He forfeited his place in the Kingdom of God. He had a place of honor and a place of privilege and a place of authority, and he rebelled and forfeited it.

When you rebel against God, you forfeit the opportunities He would give you. And Satan's agenda is to get you to rebel, and he'll use the same methodology he's used so many times before because it's been so effective.

He'll challenge God's Word. He'll challenge God's authority. "If You're the Son of God."

I don't know about you, but I have little messages that fire off in my head. I'm so old I used to call them tapes—I know nobody uses tapes anymore. And you have to learn to monitor those messages. You have to put God's Word in your heart so you can get God's Word to be the message that fires in your head. Because you'll read your Bible and the little messages go, "Do you really believe that? Are you really so old fashioned? Are you really so antiquated?" And my answer is, "I believe God."

What I don't want you to miss is Jesus was led—Jesus was led by the Spirit into the wilderness for a season that was not easy.

Jesus came to the earth certainly for a redemptive purpose to die on a cross and be raised to life. He came to bear our sin. But there's a broader understanding of why He came. The Bible says He came to give us a revelation of God. It says that in the past God spoke to us by the prophets. He spoke to us through His creation. But in Jesus He spoke to us through His son.

Jesus is the story of the Son of God incarnate. It's the story of the Son of God coming to the earth and getting an earth suit. What is the revelation that a son can give you that no one else can give you? Who can the son help you get to know better than anybody else could help you get to know them? The Father.

The revelation Jesus brought to us was of God as our Father.

In fact, Jesus said, "No one comes to the Father except through me." He said, "In my Father's house there are many rooms." Jesus gives us a revelation of God as Father. That's a very important premise.

Father, God—it's not arbitrary; it's not patriarchal. It's not to diminish women. Don't go there. It's to help us understand the nature of our relationship with God and His heart toward us.

Our Bible says in Hebrews that Jesus learned obedience through the things that He suffered. Jesus had to learn obedience. The Son of God had to learn obedience.

It says in Hebrews 12 that God disciplines those He loves—that if He doesn't discipline us, we're illegitimate children. Now, again, He doesn't break our legs to teach us lessons. God is not a child abuser. But I would submit to you that there are some things God is interested in. God as your Father is interested in holiness in you and me. He's interested in things like obedience in you and in me. Self-discipline. Purity.

Being a Christ-follower—being a child of Almighty God—does not mean that Almighty God is fully invested in every moment of your life being happy. Now He's not opposed to happiness, but He hasn't made it the primary objective.

God would lead you by His Spirit into seasons—into places—where you will listen and cooperate with Him and your character will be changed. He loves you. He will lead you through. Don't give up your hope. He hasn't abandoned you. He hasn't failed you.

In all these instances that we will look at, God uses people. God may have been involved in leading the Hebrews out, but it sure looked like their opponent was Pharaoh and an Egyptian army and slave masters with whips. It was hard to see that the opposition to them was spiritual. And in your life I suspect it's hard to see that the opposition could be anything other than a person or an organization or an institution.

But watch the outcome of Jesus' time in the wilderness. Verse 13:

> *When the devil had finished every temptation, he left Him until an opportune time. And Jesus returned to Galilee in the power of the Spirit...*
>
> LUKE 4:13-14 (NASB®)

What's our theme? *Unleashing the Power of the Holy Spirit.* Jesus came away from baptism. He came out of the wilderness in the power of the Spirit. Now watch the outcome.

> *And news about Him spread through all the surrounding district. And He began teaching in their synagogues and was praised by all.*
>
> LUKE 4:14-15 (NASB®)

Now, Jesus has lived in Galilee for almost thirty years and He's anonymous—nobody knows Him. Everybody thinks He's just another one of Mary and Joe's kids. He has no reputation; He's thirty years old.

And He makes the trip to the Jordan River and He's baptized. Then He's forty days in the wilderness, and He comes back to Galilee, Luke says, "in the power of the Spirit." Now the news about Him spreads through the whole region, and He begins teaching in their synagogues. The fuse has been lit. The power has been unleashed. He's prepared. It's time.

One of the great battles we have, I think, in following the Lord and following God's direction in our lives, is His sense of timing. When do I want God to move? Now! Really, I wanted Him to move before, but if I've had to wait until now—now is when I want Him to move.

I'm like a little kid. Have you ever seen a little kid trying to get their parents' attention? "Mommy, Mommy, Mommy." Ever been in the grocery store when that's going on? "Mommy, Mommy." Mommy's trying to shop. She's got four other kids, the phone's ringing, she's texting three people. And there's this little person going, "Mommy, Mommy..." I want to go over and say, "Please, for Pete's sake, talk to your child. Just make it stop." The kids couldn't care less what Mommy's trying to do; they're not interested in dinner. They don't care about the menu. They don't care about her timeline. They don't care about the other kids. They want attention!

I'm like that with the Lord. *So there's a few billion people on the planet, TALK TO ME!*

When our days are spent and our strength is gone, I would submit to you what we want more than anything else is to hear Almighty God say, "Well done. Well done."

The best I know at this point in my life is—if you're following

Him, if you're following His direction, you don't need to get heated up about your timeline. God has the ability—in a moment, in a day, in whatever time He needs—to accomplish His purposes.

You want Him to say, "Well done."

So don't pick up the anxiety from your timeline. Let's lay it down today and say, *Lord I trust You. Holy Spirit, You're welcome in my life. I don't want to be a rebel. I want to cooperate.* God will lead you through it.

If I could give you one last suggestion—If you're walking through one of those dry seasons, don't you stop. Don't you stop. Don't give up your hope.

I'm amazed. It makes me smile every time I read that he kept the Israelites' feet from swelling. God cares about your feet. He does. You understand how staggering that is? The most people-centric purpose of a person you know—the most generous, the most kind-hearted person—is still very limited in how much care they can really give. If you think about your own sphere of influence—yourself, your immediate family, the people that would stand in that next circle—you can't go very far and still have concern at a very deep level.

I mean, you're my friends, and you matter to me. But honestly, I didn't get up this morning worried whether or not you ate or you had a drink of water. And I confess I didn't give the first thought to your feet. I didn't, because there's just not enough of me. I'm so limited. I'm limited in my ability. I'm limited in my strength, I'm limited in my compassion. Even if you wanted, you just can't, there's not enough. True?

God took the whole crew and He said, "I've got your clothes and your water and your food and your health and your feet. I care about it. I got this," He said. It lets me know I'm good with Him. He'll get me through. And He'll bring you through.

I'd like to pray for you. We're welcoming the Holy Spirit as we've never welcomed Him before without reservation, without hesitation. We're not dictating. We're simply saying we want to cooperate. We'll follow.

PRAYER: Father, I thank You that You care for us and lead us. Lord, we welcome You into our lives as never before.

Holy Spirit, we want to welcome You. We want to cooperate with You. Forgive us when we have rejected You; forgive us when we have been unkind.

We turn our hearts and our faces to You to lay down our rebellion—where we have been stubborn and demanded our own way and ignored You.

Lord, we are sorry. We repent and we turn away from that rebellion. Lord, whether it's in our hearts, our homes, in our service to You, in our places of employment, as children or parents, whatever role it may be where we have stood as rebels,

Lord, we turn away from it today.

Forgive us. Holy Spirit help us. Just as You delivered the Hebrews from slavery, deliver us, Lord.

I pray especially for those today that are standing in desert places. Dry places. Places of limited resource. Help us to recognize Your direction and Your leading. Help us not to be shaken when we face temptation. Help us to stand. I thank You that You will lead us through those places with greater power in our lives than we've ever known before—that You will bring us into a new destination, into lands that flow with milk and honey into new seasons of opportunity. I praise You for it.

I thank You that You care for us, that You care for our provision, that You care for our well-being. Lord, that You even care about the condition of our feet. We thank You for it. We trust You today. I pray that not one of us would be turned aside, that not one would shrink back, that not one would give up. In Jesus' name, amen.

THE DESERT PLACES PART II

My agenda is simple. It's to encourage you to lay down any preconceptions—any barrier, any conclusions you have formed about limits that you intend to place on the activity of the Spirit of God in your life. It's not helpful. I appreciate our different traditions. I love the diversity that it brings to a congregation, but traditions of people and traditions of religious organizations should not keep us from cooperating with the Spirit of God. And so I'll continue to extend that invitation to you. Making a decision in your heart does not promise an outcome. Making that decision in your heart simply enables you to step through a doorway of possibility. If you don't make that decision—if you don't determine to cooperate with the Holy Spirit in that way— it's almost a certainty that your journey as a Christ-follower will remain predominantly intellectual. We need the help of the Holy Spirit to experience the things of God. I'm not opposed to our intellect. I've spent my life studying and hope to continue to do so, but I want my faith to be more than a collection of information. If that's all that's required, my computer is the most spiritual thing I own. It contains multiple versions of the Bible. I can run references in fractions of a second. But we have the opportunity for the Spirit of the Living God to indwell us, to teach us, to direct us, to lead us—what a privilege.

So far we have kind of walked through the opening doors of that, and we tried to deconstruct some of the points of fear that often are part of a journey. We tried to identify some of the invitations, the commands that Jesus gave us with respect to the Holy Spirit. And in the last chapter we began to unpack this idea of the Spirit of God moving and leading us into "desert places." We used the physical desert of Israel and the many remarkable things that have happened there with some of God's people as a template to remind us that we can be in a desert that's not physical. We go through seasons of our lives which seem to be very arid places—places where the resources are minimal.

It's really hard to imagine a desert if you've never visited one. You know, I look through the window and see fifty different shades of green. I mean, I don't have the language to describe all the colors of green that we see. If I could pick you up and deposit you south of the Dead Sea, you wouldn't need any words for green. None—you would need some words for brown and gray, and you would need a new menu of words for hot, because the ones you have are inadequate. People say to me, "It's a dry heat." So is an oven, and it feels like an oven. You feel as if you're just baking, and so it's just hard to imagine the barrenness of the desert. I've come to love it. I truly do. I enjoy being in the desert. I like the heat. There's something about it I've really come to appreciate. I like the stillness of the desert. It's remarkable.

I'll tell you a story, even though it has nothing to do with the lesson. There's a valley that runs from Jerusalem to Jericho, and it's been heavily traveled for millennia. In it there's a water channel that's been there since the first century or thereabouts. The valley is called Wadi Qelt, and years ago we hiked it from Jerusalem. It's downhill all the way to Jericho. It's only about eighteen miles or so, so it's not overwhelming. But there are a lot of cliffs and canyons, and a lot of up and down, and it's really hot, and the air's pretty still because you're down in a canyon. You're not on top, so you've got to climb. And we'd made this journey, taken the better part of a day, and we were exhausted. We scaled the last cliff and we get to the bottom of the valley, and there's a little kid about twelve years old standing with a burrow, and it has two packs on either side filled with ice and cold drinks. I'd have paid him $1000 for one drink. It was profit in the Middle East at its best. How he knew we were coming, when we would be done, I don't know. But he knew we would want whatever he had that was packed in ice. He could have been an angel for all I cared.

If you're walking through one of those seasons in the desert, or you know someone who's walking through one of those seasons—you're really my intended target. We all go through them. Nobody makes the journey without them. There are places where there's an opportunity for unparalleled fruitfulness in your spiritual life—in your relationship with the Lord. But they're often not pleasant places.

I. INTO THE DESERT (IN SCRIPTURE)

I think one of the great misunderstandings we have as God's children is that we think God's only agenda is to lead us in pleasant places. You can't arrive at that conclusion from reading the Bible. You have to ignore enormous parts of Scripture. The reality, in my understanding, is God isn't as interested in us always being in pleasant places, as He is in us maturing and growing up in Him. Sometimes life brings us challenges. Life is harder than we wish it were, and if you're walking through one of the seasons, you're not a failure. God has not abandoned you. It doesn't mean you're evil. It could be God loves you so much that He brings you to a place where His discipline is enacted upon your life. Discipline isn't always punitive. It's a mistake to think of discipline predominantly as something that is punishment. Discipline is about bringing boundaries to your life and responses to your life that weren't there previously. And when it says that God disciplines those He loves, it doesn't mean He just spanks us. It isn't just chastisement. It's that God will bring boundaries so you will lay down some of the latitude that you carried and choose a new season of focus and a heightened awareness and a different kind of an effort. You come out of a season of discipline with a different imagination of where the boundaries are. That's what discipline does. God loves you, and He disciplines you. If He doesn't discipline you, you're not His child.

Now discipline does not seem pleasant at the time—ever. Right? What's the old line? "This hurts me more than it hurts you." You never believe that if you're the one receiving that, right? And so if that's the season you're in, I pray that you come out transformed, that you will hear God's direction for your own life. In fact, I would submit to you that in the desert the Holy Spirit is often the catalyst for that part of the journey.

II. MOSES AND HEBREW PEOPLE

We looked at Moses and the Hebrew people and their journey into the desert. God led them there with a pillar of cloud and a pillar of fire. I want to note it that not everybody that goes into the desert comes out with a God-experience, and the fact that you're walking through a desert season does not mean you're coming out with a God-experience. What you do in that season determines what God can do in you and through you. Please don't miss that. A desert season is a season of opportunity, but it's not a season of certainty. Choosing the Lord with your whole heart, with your whole mind, with your whole soul, with your whole body is an important part of being a Christ-follower. We don't just make a God-decision at the point of conversion. We make God-decisions on a daily basis in the context of our life and every aspect of our life. Are we honoring God? Don't wait for the big, obvious God-decisions. Don't wait for Goliath to bellow his challenge or the army to pin you against the shores of the sea before you start to sort out what it looks like to be a godly person. Decide to make godly decisions every day of your life. If you're walking through a desert season, know this: Right now is the best time to stop and assess again your choices with regard to the Lord—to analyze the condition of your heart.

III. JESUS

Take Psalm 51—it's David's wonderful psalm of repentance—and pray it for yourself. Humble yourself. Don't imagine that you're there because of the evil in someone else's life or the wickedness in the world. Jesus was led by the Holy Spirit in the wilderness where He was tempted by Satan. But He came out of that wilderness and out of that season in the power of the Spirit, and the next season of His life was dramatically different than any season that preceded it.

The overwhelming majority—ninety-nine and nine-tenths of the Hebrew people that Moses led out of Egypt into the Wilderness—perished in the Wilderness. They didn't perish because of a lack of God's provision, a lack of God's oversight, or a lack of God's interest. He fed them daily. He provided water. He was their physician. Their clothing didn't wear out. He protected them from their enemies. It's the most remarkable thing—no generation that I'm aware of in biblical history, or in our history as a people, ever experienced more consistently the sustaining and miraculous power of God than that Exodus Generation. Yet it says that in their stubborn unbelief—in their rebellion—they would not cooperate with the Lord, and they had micro-lesson after micro-lesson. A group of them would rebel and the earth would open up and swallow them. And you're reading the story, if you're reading it for the first time, you think, *Well, tomorrow everybody'll line up and play fair.* And the next day, there's a new group of rebels. I mean, you've got to be pretty slow or pretty rebellious.

They get to the Promised Land and they send the spies in. The spies come back with the evidence of the produce of the abundance of the land, and they say, "It true. It's a land that flows with milk and honey. But there are giants in the land, and we're like grasshoppers in their sight." And Joshua and Caleb pleaded with them. They said, "Don't do this. The same God that decimated Egypt fed you manna this morning, and He'll deliver them into your hands." And they said, "No."

If the Spirit of God leads you into that season, it's to give you an opportunity to choose God in a new way. It's a precious time. Maybe not a pleasant time, but God loves you enough to lead you to an unpleasant season so that He can give you a season that's beyond anything you could imagine.

We have to reevaluate what we've thought of our faith a bit. You know, the truth is we've set Christianity aside in our culture. A lot of us have lived such blessed lives—such affluent, stable lives—lives of such remarkable security—because of where we are on Planet Earth, that we've thought all of those things were givens. We called those things rights. We've never imagined that our security and our food and our provision and our protection were extended to us from Almighty God, and so it's enabled us to have a rather bizarre presentation of Christianity where we think that it can maybe work out our eternal destination. And we can quibble about which translation of the Bible we read and what the presenter at the front of the room should wear and, you know, what our favorite theological subset of scriptures are. But we really don't invite God into the things that are the real passions of our lives. We don't invite Him into the resource accumulation of our lives. We don't invite Him into our family systems and how we should act.

The reason the Church is having such a horrific problem responding to the sexual debates of this generation is that we've ignored God's sexual boundaries for decades prior to this. And now we find ourselves at this far end of the discussion, and we are without any authority because we've ignored God's boundaries for decades.

What I'm inviting you to is an imagination where God is engaged in your life—His Spirit is involved with you to let His purposes come through you, His character be formed in you. You'll have to have a desire for the character of God to be formed in you more than you have a desire for anything else that this world has to offer.

God designed you for a life so remarkable that the only way of fulfilling your destiny is cooperating with Him. Your strength alone will not enable you to complete God's assignment. I need His help!

We don't hear that message a lot. We don't aspire to that a lot. Parents don't aspire to that for their children. If you listen to parents—if you listen to the interaction they have with their children, you find out what's in our hearts. Because their aspirations for their children are a revelation of what's in our own hearts. Again, not evil, not right and wrong—we're growing up. We're maturing in the Lord. Not attaching shame to it, I'm saying we've had a misunderstanding of our faith and we said we could recite a prayer, sit in a particular building for a few minutes on the weekends when it was convenient for us, and Almighty God—the Creator the Universe, the One that imagined everything in our world and gave us a place in it—would be thrilled that we would tip Him with a moment of our awareness and a bit of our time. It's nonsense. He said, "We will love Him with our whole heart, mind, soul, and body." We will offer ourselves, in Romans, it says as "living sacrifices." It's a paradox. It's a little blind to us, because we're not engaged with the sacrificial system. If you were accustomed to the sacrificial system, an animal was presented to the priest to offer as a sacrifice. They would slaughter the animal, and the carcass would go on the altar. By the time the carcass goes on the altar, it is void of any self-determination. It doesn't hop up and say, "Oh, it's hot," any more than your steak jumps off the grill. And Paul is using that image, and he says, "Offer yourself as a sacrifice." But he slips in that little word "living." Offer your life as a sacrifice to God. He says that's our "reasonable" expression of worship. That's not some hyper kind of a Christian.

You see, I would submit to you we have a little business to do with God before we get to that place. We have to talk to Him rather candidly and say, "Lord, I haven't really been interested in that. I've been interested in my own agenda. I've been interested in Your power helping me get more of what I want." And I don't think God is opposed to that, but it's not His primary agenda in our lives. So those desert seasons—uncomfortable, awkward, sometimes minimalistic, seasons of realignment, seasons when you can choose to imagine that God has invited you there—

are seasons of tremendous opportunity. While the generation that left Egypt and went into the wilderness didn't occupy the Promised Land, their children did. There's hope in that.

IV. JOHN THE BAPTIST

Not everyone who went into the wilderness to see John the Baptist responded to him positively. Apparently, large numbers of people went and repented and were baptized. But the religious leaders from Jerusalem, when they got there—John calls them a "brood of vipers." He said, "Who warned you to flee?" They're there to monitor what's happening. They're there to look. They're observers. They're kind of like UN officials. I've been to a few places in the world where there were global conflicts, and the UN trucks and the white cars show up. In those places they're usually referred to by the locals as the "United Nothing." They're there to observe. They don't intend to participate. They're there to gather facts and to report. They don't really have any skin in the game. The outcome isn't particularly relevant to them. Their home is someplace else, and oftentimes we have observed the things of the Lord with kind of that United Nations approach. Our home is someplace else. We're not overly invested in this, but we're just curious. Now curiosity might bring you to the table and cause you to take a look, but at some point you have to decide you're going to yield your life and be a Christ-follower.

V. ELIJAH

I want to pick up a couple more examples. One is Elijah. I can tell most of this story without reading it. You know Elijah was a prophet. A part of his ministry took place during the time of King Ahab and Jezebel. Ahab is the Gold Standard for wickedness. What a way to make the Book. He's married to a Phoenician queen who is more wicked than he is—a witch, in the biblical sense of that word. Together, they have a powerful influence over the nation. Ultimately, Elijah confronts the people and makes them choose between their idol worship and worshipping God—you know the story. They meet on Mount Carmel, and fire falls from heaven. It's one of the more dramatic Bible stories we have. Then Elijah slaughters the priests of Baal. I mean, it's not a kids' story, but it's a turning of the nation, and at the fulcrum—at the front of that is Elijah willing to stand up and say, "There is a God." You know, in our generation, we're going to have to have the courage to stand up and say, "There is a God." There's a consequence to that. There is. It's time. We've hidden behind in our churches and sung our choruses and then gone out into the world and done business and acted like we couldn't spell Jesus. We've been wrong. We are Christ-followers 24/7. You can't compartmentalize your faith and imagine it's valid.

Do you remember what happened to the Israelites after their victory at the Red Sea? What was their next stop? Marah.

It's the word that means "bitter." God led them from the tremendous victory of the Red Sea to a place where the water was bitter. After Elijah's tremendous victory on Mount Carmel, 1 Kings 19:3 says, "Elijah was afraid and ran for his life." Do you know why? Jezebel said, "I'll take his head tomorrow. I'll do to him tomorrow what he did to my prophets today." And the man who prayed and fire fell from the sky was afraid and ran for his life. You're reading this story, and you think, *Dude, if you can call fire out of the sky, just put Jezebel's name on the list.* But it's not always that simple. You have to expand your imagination a little bit. The most remarkable people of God still face challenges that frighten them. I don't believe Elijah was weak. I don't believe he was cowardly. I don't believe he was uninformed. I think he's a powerful window into our own selves. We can have tremendous victories and be so spent emotionally, physically—in every way—that we're vulnerable to those threats. So he runs, and guess where he runs to? The desert.

Mount Carmel is at the northern end of a mountain chain, and, at least what is considered the traditional site of that event, juts out into the ocean—into the Mediterranean. It was a landmark for the sailors for a long time. They navigated along the coast of that end of the Mediterranean. He leaves the green, the more lush part of Israel, and he runs into the desert to Beersheba in Judah. Beersheba is south of Jerusalem—a journey that takes several days. He left his servant there, and went a day's journey further into the desert. And he came to a tree, sat down under it, and he prayed that he might die. He said, "I've had enough, Lord. I've just had enough. I've stood for You. It's all I want. Take my life. I'm not better than my ancestors." He lay down under the tree and he fell asleep, and an angel touched him and said, "Get up and eat." It's almost the same language as, "How are your feet?" I love it. There's such a personal notion to it, and please don't miss that if you're walking through that season, because when I'm in those seasons, I think, *God, You must be mad at me. You must be disappointed in me. You must be somehow withdrawn from me, or You wouldn't have put me in this place.* And yet when I find all of those desert places, the Lord is close to the people. He's feeding them. He's taking care of their feet. He's cooking for them. He's not far from you. He has an imagination for you beyond where you are, beyond what you have for yourself.

Finally, the Lord speaks to Elijah. In verse 13, it says,

> *When Elijah heard it, he pulled his cloak over his face and went out and stood at the mouth of the cave. Then a voice said to him, "What are you doing here, Elijah?"*

1 KINGS 19:13

Now you can tell the depth of Elijah's despair because he doesn't relent easily. He said, "I have been very zealous for the LORD God Almighty. The Israelites have rejected your covenant, broken down your altars, and put your prophets to death with the sword." So far he's told the truth, and then he adds to it his feelings. Your emotions will take you some places that are not always helpful. He said, "I am the only one left, and now they are trying to kill me too." He got everything right except that one little slip, because they were trying to kill him—and that's not a pleasant place. You know, if they're trying to kill you, you feel like you're the only one, right?

The LORD said to him, "Go back the way you came, and go to the Desert of Damascus."

1 KINGS 19:15

Now Damascus is north of Israel—at the top end of the Golan Heights—same Damascus we know today.

"When you get there, anoint Hazael king over Aram. And... anoint Jehu...king over Israel, and anoint Elisha...to succeed you as prophet."

1 KINGS 19:15-16

You know what God just did? He just did a regime change. He said, "Elijah, you stood up on Mount Carmel and the people repented, and now you're hiding in the desert." He said, "Get up, and here's your assignment—anoint a new king over the nation. He will overthrow the king that you battle, take his place in the land of Israel, and a new prophet will occupy the office that you have stood in."

He came out with a complete victory and got the whole thing. But it isn't because he feels triumphant. He isn't even filled with joy. He is exhausted in every way, and God meets him there. Hear it—there is no condemnation. Look at the last line. He said, "I reserve seven thousand in Israel—all whose knees have not bowed down to Baal and all whose mouths have not kissed him." We don't know exactly the population. Seven thousand's not a lot of people. It's a tiny percentage of the larger population of the nation. Being a Christ-follower will often put you in a minority. We've got to recalibrate a little bit how we think. We do. We have to value one another more. There's another believer in the place where you work? Thank God for them. Don't be critical of them because they read the King James and you read The Message or the reverse. We've got to have a little recalibration inwardly. There's no criticism from God for Elijah. There's no condemnation from Him, but God in His grace and His mercy says, "Elijah, you haven't failed. There's a whole new season ahead, with a whole different direction. Your courage, the place you've stood, is going to result in a different future." Elisha, who succeeds him, does twice—you can count them—twice the number of miracles that Elijah did. Elisha asks for a double portion of the anointing on Elijah, and he receives it. And if you're in that place, there's something good ahead of you.

VI. DAVID

I'll give you one more—David. He's arguably the greatest king of all the Israelite kings—but also a man with great flaws. You know the story, but for our discussion I'm more interested in this moment in his journey from 1 Samuel chapter 16. There's already a king when David is anointed to be king. God sends Samuel to his house:

> *So he sent and had him brought in. He was ruddy, with a fine appearance and handsome features. ...the LORD said, "Rise and anoint him; he is the one." So Samuel took the horn of oil and anointed him in the presence of his brothers, and from that day on the Spirit of the LORD came upon David in power.*
>
> 1 SAMUEL 16:12-13

There's that association again—the Spirit of the Lord and the power of God.

If you are dependent upon the power of God for an outcome in your life, you have no choice but to make peace with the Person of the Holy Spirit. As long as you have a barrier there of any description, you are walling yourself off from the power of God. It's not a prudent choice. Humble yourself.

Samuel anoints him, and it says that the Spirit of the Lord came on David in power, and Samuel goes on. Now if you're just reading this for the first time, you think David is going to move from here to the palace. But most of you know his story, and that's far from true. He has years before he will ascend to the throne of Israel. There's a king already there—a jealous king. In fact, there are some interesting parallels between David's story and Joseph's story. As young men, they have a window—God gives them a vision into what their future is. Joseph is met with the jealousy of his brothers and ends up being sold into slavery in Egypt and betrayed. You know, that's a difficult journey. David isn't betrayed by his brothers, but he faces the jealousy of King Saul and the false accusation and the attempts to destroy him and everything that he has. And David's place of refuge, by now I hope you would imagine, is the desert. He flees into the desert, and it's in the desert where David becomes a celebrated leader of men. It's in the desert where he gathers his "mighty men" around him. It's in the desert where his exploits and his fame really grow and build. I mean, he has the Goliath-challenge as a young man, but he's a one-hit-wonder with Goliath if he doesn't have the rest of the story to go with it. And all of that takes place in the desert while he's a fugitive. When you read the Psalms, you can hear it: "But God, You sent the prophet. I didn't go to the prophet. I didn't submit my name on the list. I didn't ask to be anointed. I didn't volunteer for the assignment. You sent him to my house, and now I'm in the desert because of a choice You made." There are times when standing for the truth, when owning your faith, will put you in a place that's not comfortable. Do it anyway. You don't have to be obnoxious or condemning or critical or narrow-minded. I'm not talking about that. I'm just saying own the truth—say, "Yes, I am for Jesus."

It was in the desert where the real remarkable part of the David-story was born. In fact, I studied at Hebrew University, and I had a class on "Kingship in Ancient Israel" focused on David's life. The professor was a Jewish religious man with a tender heart for God, and with tears in his eyes, I remember him saying, "The most remarkable part of David's life took place up until the point that he took the city of Jerusalem." And he said, "After that, his track record really wasn't so good." It was in the desert where the power of God in his life was the most evident. When the options were fewer and he was dependent upon the presence of God—that was where he had the most remarkable influence. The relationships that carried him for the rest of his life were all built and born in this season in the desert. Cooperate with the Lord. Humble yourself.

He's the greatest king in Israelite history. Three thousand years after David's gone, I can tell you this: The enemies of the Jewish people in the land of Israel today still hate King David. They do their best to destroy any archaeological evidence that he existed. Now I'm here to tell you, you're one bad dude if 3,000 years after you're gone, your enemies are still fighting about you. Serve the Lord with a heart in such a way that people opposed to God's purposes in the earth would just want to deny you exist. That's the truth.

VII. TRAVEL TIPS FOR DESERT CROSSING

Let me give you some travel tips if you're crossing the desert. Now this is not rocket science, and it's an abbreviated list. If you want a fun desert story and just a little window into the extremes of the desert, go back and read the book of Jonah. I know Jonah is a fish story, but Jonah ends in the desert. Just read the last chapter of Jonah. After Jonah's done with Nineveh, he goes out and sits down on a hillside because he wants to watch the destruction. What a happy prophet he was. He wasn't intending for Nineveh to repent. He didn't want Nineveh to thrive. He was politically astute enough to know that if Nineveh thrived and Assyria flourished, they were coming for his homeland. And he was quite content for them to be destroyed. So he goes and sits down on a hillside, and it says that God caused a vine to grow, and the vine provided shade for Jonah. And he was so happy about the vine, because shade in the desert makes all the difference. Trust me. It says God provided the vine, and then it says God provided a worm. It was discipline for Jonah. He wasn't punishing Jonah. He was tightening Jonah's perspective. The worm ate the vine and the vine wilted, and he was exposed to the sun and he got so angry, he said to God, "I'm so mad I could just die." And God said, "Jonah, you're angry about a worm and a vine, but you couldn't care less about the people of Nineveh."

Do you have any imagination that God can use you when your heart isn't just exactly right? I hope you do, or you're letting the

Devil rob from you many, many productive days in the Kingdom of God. God doesn't use us because we're perfect. He works through our lives because He loves us. God's desire to help people is so great, He will speak through a donkey. That's how I get to the podium. So don't let the Devil berate you because of the inconsistencies of your life. I'm not encouraging you to be sloppy, but don't let the Devil rob you. You're not in the desert because you're imperfect. You're in the desert because God loves you, and He's delivering you. He's bringing you to a better place—if you'll cooperate with Him. If you stand in your rebellion, you'll spend your time in the desert.

A. SHADE & WATER

Shade and water—you need both when you're in the desert. Without them, life is miserable. You won't survive. You just won't. In chapter 7 of John's Gospel, Jesus is in Jerusalem. It's a desert city. You can't get to Jerusalem without going through the desert.

> *On the last and greatest day of the Feast, Jesus stood and said in a loud voice, "If anyone is thirsty, let him come to me and drink."*
>
> JOHN 7:37

I promise you, in Jerusalem, everybody's thirsty. Water is the most precious resource in the Middle East today, and it was in antiquity. The wars in the Middle East are fought over water, and Jesus stands up and says in a loud voice, "Anybody thirsty? I've got water." Everybody looks. Everybody listens. Everybody leans in. He says,

> *"Whoever believes in me, as the Scripture has said, streams of living water will flow from within him."*
>
> JOHN 7:38

Now that's Jesus statement. Verse 39 is John's commentary. John wrote this Gospel after the Jesus-story—after Jesus' return to Heaven. He is writing this in retrospect. He's giving you Jesus' statement, but then He says to us, from hindsight:

> *By this he meant the Spirit, whom those who believed in him were later to receive. Up to that time the Spirit had not been given, since Jesus had not yet been glorified.*
>
> JOHN 7:39

John uses Jesus' words to help us understand that He meant the "streams of living water" from within us was the Spirit of God. Unleashing the power of the Holy Spirit is important! Jesus just made the invitation to everybody on the Temple Mount. The Spirit isn't poured out on those that are perfect or fully obedient. One of the mistakes we make is we think that the Spirit of God only works through people who have accomplished some level of purity or purification or heightened something or other. The reality is, God works through us in all of our imperfections.

I've said many times, and I'm sure I will repeat it again: You have to guard your heart. The fruit of the Spirit is the evidence that someone is cooperating with the Spirit of God. You know the fruit of the Spirit from Galatians 5: love, joy, peace, patience, goodness... You have to cooperate with the Spirit of God to let those things emerge in your character. The gifts of the Spirit, the manifestations of the Spirit, the expressions of the power of the Spirit of God are not character-based. The fruit of the Spirit is the insulation for the manifestations, for the gifts of the Spirit. But we tend to attach maturity to persons where we see manifestations of the power of God. It's a bad choice. You want to look for the fruit of the Spirit. That is evidence of the character being yielded to the Spirit of God. God's desire to help people is so great as I said a moment ago, He'll do supernatural things through a donkey. Don't follow people because you see the supernatural. It's not evidence of maturity—it's evidence of the grace of God. Look for the fruit of the Spirit. It's not either or. We need both. Psalm 91 says,

He who dwells in the shelter of the Most High will rest in the shadow of the Almighty.

PSALM 91:1

I love that—there's something so personal about this whole desert idea—that God cares about the food you eat. He cares about your physical strength. He cares about the condition of your feet. He's concerned about the temperature that you're thriving in. He'll provide shade for you. It's so personal. He understands it's an awkward season. He understands it's not an optimal season. But you're not abandoned. You're not alone. He hasn't forgotten you.

One more scripture, from Psalm 121:

> *The LORD is your keeper; the LORD is your shade on your right hand. The sun will not smite you by day, nor the moon by night. The LORD will protect you from all evil; He will keep your soul. The LORD will guard your going out and your coming in from this time forth and forever.*
>
> PSALM 121:5-8, NASB®

B. VALUE OF A GOOD GUIDE

In the desert, a good guide is invaluable. He's just invaluable. In John 16 and verse 12, Jesus said,

> *"When he, the Spirit of truth, comes, he will guide you into all truth."*
>
> JOHN 16:13

Folks, cooperating with the Holy Spirit is a good idea. You know, I don't know how many tours I have participated in to Israel. I went the first time when I was in the sixth grade. I studied there—lived there for a season—and when I studied there I didn't have access to the guides. I had access to a library and local knowledge. I even learned the language enough I could get by on the street. But you know, I'd spend the day walking the streets of Jerusalem, and I'd see things and I'd have to go back to the library and look them up and try to figure out what I'd seen and what it was. On the other hand, if you can spend a half a day with somebody that knows the city, knows what you're looking at, that's providing an explanation, that helps you find the shortcuts, who knows where the good food is—it totally changes the experience. People say, "I just wish I had the time to go there by myself and drive around." You'd waste most of your days. You'd visit some parts of Israel that would not be a blessing. A good guide makes all the difference. Trust me. It's true spiritually as well. You can live with the attitude of "me do it," or you can cooperate with the Helper. How many times have you heard that from children, right? If they can touch it, if they can get it to their mouth, "Me wants to do it." We don't really outgrow that. We just get more sophisticated at hiding it. Or we can say to the Spirit of God, "Help me," and He will.

I want to close this section with Revelation 1. I thought it was such a good example. The Apostle John is in a desert, but of a different kind. He's an old man. His peer group is gone. Peter's gone, James is gone, and Andrew is gone. He's been banished to an island. It's really just not an optimal place, and he's not there because he's a thief or he's immoral. He's there because he's been an advocate for Jesus. He says,

I, John, your brother and companion in the suffering and kingdom and patient endurance that are ours in Jesus, was on the island of Patmos because of the word of God and the testimony of Jesus.

REVELATION 1:9

Doesn't that sound like a desert trip? He said, "I'm suffering, and I'm enduring patiently."

On the Lord's Day I was in the Spirit, and I heard behind me a loud voice like a trumpet...

REVELATION 1:10

And when he turns to look, who does he see? Jesus. He said, "I fell at his feet like I was dead." But to me, the key to the whole book—the whole remarkable story of Revelation, is what John says in verse 10: "It was the Lord's Day, and I was in the Spirit." I think of all the other places he could have been. I think of all the other things he could have given himself to, but he says, "I was in the Spirit." Folks, our choices do make a difference, and your attitude towards the Person of the Holy Spirit is important.

We need His help. He is for your good. He will not embarrass you or humiliate you or diminish you. He doesn't want to take anything from you. You don't have anything He needs. He wants to help you. I want to be all in with Him.

PRAYER: Heavenly Father, I rejoice in Your faithfulness. You have chosen a path for me that leads to righteousness and complete fulfillment. I trust Your provision for my life. You are my security. You watch over my days. My life is a testimony to the power of my God—a declaration of Your great love. Holy Spirit, direct my path to a place of triumph. Deliver me from every snare. I will rest in the shadow of Your protection. Let the name of Jesus be lifted high. Amen.

UNLEASHING THE POWER OF THE HOLY SPIRIT

CLOTHED WITH POWER

In the places in your life where you need the power of God to help you—if you've imagined an outcome that you can't orchestrate on your own and you've invited God to be a help to you—it's impossible to imagine that power of God apart from the Spirit of God. So if you have a desire for God's power to help you, whether you're conscious of it or not, you're really extending an invitation to the Holy Spirit to help you. And if you begin with preconditions and limits on the Person of the Holy Spirit—concerning how you'll welcome Him, or how you'll cooperate with Him, or what you'll allow Him to do—you are in effect limiting the power of God that's available to your life. That's not prudent.

On a typical weekend at World Outreach Church, we come from more than 60 different Christian traditions—all the way from orthodox churches to people who have never been to a church before. That means we've had a lot of diverse training, input, and rhetoric on the Person and the work of the Holy

Spirit. That's not necessarily a bad thing. I happen to think it strengthens the community of faith. But I would encourage you to come to a conclusion amongst yourselves for a very simple invitation. Something like this: *Holy Spirit, You're welcome in my life*—period. No preconditions, no preconceptions, no limits, no demands—*I want to welcome You into my life without any barriers. I want Your help.* If we can arrive at that place, I believe we create an opportunity for God to move in our midst beyond anything we've ever known in our lives.

I. CLOTHED WITH POWER

Our topic is about being "Clothed with Power," and I really borrowed the phrase from Luke. It's the last phrase he gives us from Jesus. It's Luke 24:49. Jesus is speaking:

> *"I am going to send you what my Father has promised; but stay in the city until you have been clothed with power from on high."*
>
> LUKE 24:49

Some of you are pretty fashion-conscious, which is not evil, but I would submit to you being "clothed with power" is the ultimate fashion statement. Clothed with God's power—that's an intriguing image to me. Clothed with the power of God—that was Jesus' desire for His closest friends and followers, and I would submit to you it's His desire for you and me.

Luke authored the Gospel that bears his name, but he wrote one other New Testament book—the book of Acts. In the Gospel, he tells us the Jesus-story. In the book of Acts, he tells us the story of Jesus' disciples after Jesus returned to Heaven. The Gospel that bears his name is Jesus fulfilling the Mosaic Covenant. Jesus came as an observant Jewish man. He fulfilled the Mosaic Law perfectly. He met the standards of God for righteousness. The book of Acts tells us of Jesus' followers living under the authority of the New Covenant, and the imperative that Jesus gave to them was to be clothed with power. In the book of Acts, Jesus follows that up in chapter 1:

> *On one occasion, while he was eating with them, he gave them this command: "Do not leave Jerusalem, but wait for the gift my Father promised, which you have heard me speak about. For John baptized with water, but in a few days you will be baptized with the Holy Spirit." … But you will receive power when the Holy Spirit comes on you; and you will be my witnesses in Jerusalem, and in all Judea and Samaria, and to the ends of the earth."*

ACTS 1:4-5,8

Since the same person authored the Gospel of Luke and the book of Acts, we can see a constant thought—he's telling one story. The books are just broken apart because it was a two volume set. He closes Luke by saying, "You'll be clothed with power," and he opens Acts by saying, "You will receive power when the Holy Spirit comes on you; and you will be my witnesses in Jerusalem, and in all Judea and Samaria, and to the ends of the earth."

Then in Acts chapter 2 is the fulfillment of that promise—it's the day of Pentecost. Pentecost is a Jewish holiday. It has nothing to do with the theological grouping or a doctrine or a particular group of people. Pentecost is "fifty days," thus, "pente" after Passover. So it's on a Jewish holiday that God fulfilled His promise through Jesus. He sent the Holy Spirit and it stirred the whole city of Jerusalem. The disciples, when the Spirit came upon them, were speaking in languages beyond those that they'd learned (Acts 2:1-4). A crowd gathered and Peter stood up to address the crowd, and thousands of people accepted Jesus as Messiah.

Now that is the fulfillment of what Jesus commanded them to wait for. But it's the transformation that I want to draw your attention to, because that's the part that intrigues me. It's the reason for the discussion we're having. How can we cooperate with the Spirit of God? How can you and I be clothed with power? You see, I think when we think about unleashing the power of the Holy Spirit we usually think about the miraculous, the supernatural—praying for the sick and the sick get better or miracles of another description. I think that's appropriate, but I would like to expand your imagination a bit into an arena that

I think is of equal significance—that living an empowered life and being clothed with the power of God—is equally about a life transformed. The power of God is available and present to transform us—to help us break free from the practice of sin and lust that comes from a life apart from God.

We need God's power to do that. We're not going to do that just by the strength of our will. I want to set aside the notion that being a churched person, a good Christ-follower, just means you're a little tame or a little polite. Or that you've just polished up your vocabulary a little bit, or your beverage list—like you've turned the volume down on your life. Being a Christ-follower means you turn the volume all the way up and rip the knob off. Being a Christ-follower is not a diminished life. That way of thinking is a lie! The power of God that's available to you and to me isn't just that we can get a little power boost when there's a problem we don't know how to grapple with. There is a power available that will transform us. Being a Christ-follower is living a transformed life.

I know a lot of us have stepped away from that idea, because we've been invited to church and invited to worship services and they didn't feel very powerful.

But let's use Peter, since on the day of Pentecost he's the spokesperson. A few days earlier, when Jesus was arrested (and this is after three years with Jesus; he's been trained, coached by the greatest leader our world has ever known), Peter follows along behind. He wants to see what's going to happen. While warming himself at a fire a servant girl that's there sees Peter, and she says, "Aren't you one of His followers?" Peter says, "Not me. I don't know Him." A little bit later somebody's watching Peter, and they say, "You know, no, I heard the question she put to you, and I'm certain I've seen you with Jesus." And this time with profanity he says, "I've never known Him."

Now scroll forward just a few weeks—no more classes, no more training, no more ministry—just the outpouring of the Spirit in Acts chapter 2. Peter stands up in that chapter and addresses the crowd that's gathered and says,

> *"God made this Jesus from Nazareth, whom you crucified, both Lord and Messiah."*

ACTS 2:36

He's not hiding now! Later in chapter 3, he and John meet a beggar and the beggar is healed. It stirs the whole city of Jerusalem, and they're brought before the Sanhedrin.

The Sanhedrin was the Jewish ruling body. They didn't have the power to sentence someone to crucifixion—that was a Roman punishment—so they orchestrated the events and the charges to deliver Jesus to the Roman governor to be crucified.

Peter is standing before the Sanhedrin and they say, "You have filled this city with rumors about this man, Jesus." And Peter— the same Peter who a few days earlier denied he even knew Jesus—steps forward and says, "You're right. You crucified the King of Glory, and we will never stop talking about Him. You do what you've got to do." I'm paraphrasing here but it's in there. You can read it (Acts 4:1-21).

How do you explain the transformation in Peter, going from where he won't even acknowledge he knows Jesus, to standing before a group that could take his life from him and speaking with that kind of boldness? It says,

When they saw the courage of Peter and John and realized that they were unschooled, ordinary men, they were astonished and they took note that these men had been with Jesus.

ACTS 4:13

The transformational event in Peter's life that Luke makes an unmistakable part of the narrative was the outpouring of the Spirit of God. Peter was "clothed with power."

God's Spirit in you and me, will enable us to lead a different kind of a life than people that don't have His help. If there is no difference in the quality of life between a Christ-follower and a pagan, then why be a Christ-follower? Because you're so bored you don't have anything to do on the weekends? I don't think so. Let's open our hearts to the clear invitation of Scripture—that the Spirit of God will bring change to us. There is a power available beyond just the strength of our will, the force of our character, or our determination.

II. POWER TO BE GODLY

A. PROVISION

Now I want to unpack with you this notion of the power to be godly. In 2 Peter it says:

> *His divine power has given us everything we need for life and godliness through our knowledge of him who called us by his own glory and goodness.*

2 PETER 1:3

What an amazing promise—"everything we need for life and godliness." This morning when you finished your preparation for the day—getting yourself ready so you could come out in public with the rest of us—how many of you looked in the mirror and thought, *you are just so godly*—huh? Me either. It just doesn't happen, does it? In fact, you look in the mirror and you go, *I hope nobody really knows*. But the clear promise is that God has given us everything we need to be godly. He hasn't held anything back from you. You and I recognize the gulf, but there's a power available to help us.

B. HOLINESS EMPOWERS

Make every effort to live in peace with all men and to be holy;
without holiness no one will see the Lord. See to it that no
one misses the grace of God and that no bitter root grows up
to cause trouble and defile many. See that no one is sexually
immoral, or is godless like Esau, who for a single meal sold his
inheritance rights as the oldest son.

HEBREWS 12:14-16

Look at this passage, it says, "Make every effort to live in peace with all men and to be holy..." Make every effort. Underline those three little words: "Make every effort." What effort does that leave out? Not much, does it? This isn't about halfhearted or occasionally or when you're in the mood. It doesn't mean if there's nothing else happening or there's not a ballgame on or if it isn't raining. It also says, "Without holiness no one will see the Lord." Holiness is not optional. I bet while you were looking in the mirror wondering how godly you were, none of you just felt overwhelmed with holiness, did you? Do you start your day looking and go, *You holy rascal...?* Yeah, me either. But without holiness no one sees the Lord.

That's stated rather negatively. Let's flip it and state it another way—with holiness you can see the Lord. Now that intrigues me. Holiness empowers you, and I don't think we value it. I think we think of holiness, again, kind of in that diminished category—as if it turns down the volume on pleasure, fun, excitement, enthusiasm, joy or the life-experience. As if you couldn't be holy and enjoy life more. Who told you that lie? Holiness will bring good things to you. Holiness will take the lid off of your life. Do you really think that rebellion, selfishness, stubbornness, envy, pride and self-centeredness will bring you a more fulfilled life? Do you really think that unchecked immorality, brazen ungodliness and perversion will bring greater fulfillment, contentment and joy to you?

We need to process what's really on the inside of us. Holiness is a good thing. Make every effort. You may say, "Well, I don't want to go overboard." Why not? Why would you say that about the Lord? Think of the things that you wouldn't apply that thought process to.

Suppose somebody said to you, "You can make all the money you want."

"Uh, I don't want to go overboard."

"I've found this wonderful new diet! You can lose weight."

"I don't want to go overboard. I kind of like being fluffy."

"I found a way you can train your kids. They will be geniuses."

"Nah, nah, I don't want to go overboard. I like ignorant."

Where did we get this notion with the things of the Lord that we're looking for the broad middle? I want to go too far—build a ramp, back up, get some speed, and hit the edge wide open! What are you doing?

Make every effort. Holiness is good in you. I think we shy away from it because we feel that there's so little of it, and we've never recognized or acknowledged or reconciled what the scripture says. There's a power available to help us. I need power to help me be holy, because I'm not going to do it on my own.

Romans 1:4 says of Jesus,

Who through the Spirit of holiness was declared with power
to be the Son of God by his resurrection from the dead…

ROMANS 1:4

I love that line—"The spirit of holiness was declared with power." The power of God—one of the outcomes of cooperating with the Spirit that is at work in you and me is holiness, because with holiness we can see the Lord. Folks, when you see the Lord in His fullness and His majesty and in His glory, you won't have any reluctance. But right now we see through the glass darkly, and we need God's help.

C. THE HELP OF THE SPIRIT

How does the Spirit help us? It's an important question. Lets look at Genesis chapter 6, there's a flood and Noah has built a big boat for all of the animals—remember the story? Noah basically built a floating barn. I like him, but at the beginning of that chapter there is a statement:

> *Then the LORD said, "My Spirit shall not strive with man forever, because he also is flesh; nevertheless his days shall be one hundred and twenty years."*

GENESIS 6:3, NASB®

It's an interesting image. The Spirit of God in this tug of war with humanity, inviting them toward godliness as human beings. I've said to you often that the Bible is the story of Adam and his descendants—we're a race of rebels. From the beginning chapters of Genesis to the conclusion of Revelation, we rebel against the purposes of God. No matter what He does for us, no matter how supernatural, how miraculous, how abundant His provision—our default position is rebellion. But the Spirit of God intercedes with us, intervenes in us, inviting us toward the things of the Lord. You all know this. It's happened in your life; it happens in mine. But in Genesis 6 God says something that should capture your attention. He says, "My Spirit will not always do that." Then the doors get closed on the floating barn and there is total annihilation. You see, it adds a note of sobriety to this notion of cooperating with the Holy Spirit. It's no longer just an option. It's a bit more of a nudge.

1. CHALLENGING CORRUPTION

Later, in the New Testament, when Jesus is talking about His second coming during His longest prophetic discourse He makes a parallel between the days of Noah. It's why I included it here. It says,

> *"No one knows about that day or hour,* [the day or hour when He will come the second time] *not even the angels in heaven, nor the Son, but only the Father. As it was in the days of Noah, so it will be at the coming of the Son of Man. For in the days before the flood, people were eating and drinking, marrying and giving in marriage, up to the day Noah entered the ark; and they knew nothing about what would happen until the flood came and took them all away. That is how it will be at the coming of the Son of Man."*

MATTHEW 24:36-39

Wow. Jesus said there's a parallel between Noah's day and the earth prior to His return. Then He lists some characteristics. He says, "But until the ark was closed, people were eating and drinking, marrying and giving in marriage." None of those activities are immoral or wrong or wicked. They were just unconcerned about the things of God. It says they had no clue what was coming. The Bible tells us in some other places that Noah was a preacher of righteousness. For forty years he told the people what was coming. And oh, by the way, he's building a huge, floating barn in the middle of a field. But they could not have cared less. Holiness wasn't on their agenda. They weren't interested. They just wanted their way—not greatly dissimilar from the world in which we live. It says they were like this until the day came when "the flood came and took them all away." At that point there was nothing they could do.

You see, God's delay in the return of Jesus to the earth is an expression of His mercy. Because once Jesus comes back, there's no more opportunity. It's like when the door on the ark was sealed. The delay in Jesus' return is an opportunity for us to be in the harvest fields. It's an opportunity for us to take the Jesus-story to our co-workers and our neighbors and our family members and the people in our sphere of influence. But the day will come when that opportunity will close just as certainly as the door closed on the ark. In the meantime, the Spirit of God, it said in Genesis 6, strives with us. He strives with you and me, inviting us towards godliness. The Spirit of God strives with you and me to help us.

2. CONSCIENCE DULLED

If you refuse to cooperate with Him, your conscience becomes somewhat dulled or calloused to Him. Lets look at 1 Timothy:

The Spirit clearly says that in later times some will abandon the faith and follow deceiving spirits and things taught by demons. Such teachings come through hypocritical liars, whose consciences have been seared as with a hot iron. They forbid people to marry and order them to abstain from certain foods, which God created to be received with thanksgiving by those who believe and who know the truth.

1 TIMOTHY 4:1-3

In verse 1 it says, "The Spirit clearly says that in later times some will abandon the faith and follow deceiving spirits and things taught by demons." It's a pretty sobering sentence. He's talking about the season we're living in now. He says in those times there will be many people who "abandon the faith and follow deceiving spirits." They won't abandon religion or stop their God-discussions. There will still be churches, religious people, religious clothing and religious music—but they're going to abandon a faith in God. They'll be deceived. The deception will be powerful enough that they'll have demonic motivation.

Let's look at verse 2: "Such teachings come through hypocritical liars, whose consciences have been seared as with a hot iron."

That's a very powerful image, isn't it? He's using the image of skin being cauterized by great heat—being burned—to describe a conscience seared. When that happens there's damage to the tissue. The nerves are damaged so you lose sensitivity. It's painful in the moment, but the outcome is that you lose the awareness or physical sensation. If your conscience is seared, you can no longer feel when the Holy Spirit prompts you, prods you, invites you or nudges you. You can't sense when the Spirit of God is saying do this or don't do this. You and I have to make a choice to cooperate, or we just turn up the volume in our life and ignore the Spirit with cluttered noise. When you refuse to cooperate with Him, it's as if your conscience begins to callous. It becomes seared. Don't do that. The Holy Spirit is your Friend. He's your Helper. He will improve the quality of your life. He will bring the power of God to bear on your behalf to bring about transformation that you and I are powerless to bring.

You know the difference between conviction and condemnation, right? The Holy Spirit convicts us. He is our Helper, to help us understand holiness and godliness and righteousness and purity. We need this because we live in a world where there's a whole myriad of opportunities and options and we have an old earthly, carnal, ungodly self that will prompt us in the wrong direction. But we have the gift of the Holy Spirit, and He can help us navigate by prompting us with, "Oh, don't do that—don't say that." Or "Say you're sorry for saying that." Or "Humble yourself." You've all experienced that. It can come in a lot of ways. It doesn't always come mysteriously in some voice from the sky. It can come from a book or a song or a friend or something you hear, or it can come from a voice within you. But you can recognize that God-prompt.

A good thing about conviction is that it always comes with a pathway towards something better. When you feel that convicting presence of the Spirit of God, the correct response is repentance. Repentance says, "I'm wrong, and I'll choose a new direction." Sometimes the Lord will convict you about something in the past. As you grow up in the Lord—as you mature in the Lord—I find He will convict you of things in your past so that you can lay them down and shed encumbrances. Think of it in the same context as athletic training. If you haven't exercised in ten years and you start exercising, all you're really looking to do is move a little bit at first, because you've been sedate. But if you stay with it and you get a year or two into your new training protocol, now you're no longer just moving. You start doing some specified movements to target areas and bring focus to things in all kinds of ways. The same is true as you grow up in the Lord. When you become a Christ-follower, you say, "Lord, I'm a sinner and I need a savior, help me." But as you begin to mature and grow in the Lord, the Holy Spirit will help you lay aside things that have encumbered you—sometimes from your past. It could be from your childhood; it could be from your adult life. We gather junk as we move through life. When you bump into those places, cooperate with the Holy Spirit. Don't defend, excuse or justify it. Don't say, "Well, you know, that's just the way my family is." Recognize that you're in a new family now—it's called the family of God—and repent. Don't just say, "I'm sorry." Saying "I'm sorry" doesn't cover it. "I'm sorry" could just mean, "I'm sorry I got caught." "I'm sorry" could mean, "I'm sorry you're so narrow minded that you don't understand I'm right." It's almost a pity statement. Say, "Lord, I'm sorry. I want to repent. I will lay that down." That's conviction. It's a helpful thing. It's a powerful thing. It's a gift in your life.

In fact, when the Holy Spirit shines His light on an aspect of your life and illumines it and invites you to change, that is one of the most precious gifts you can ever receive. He's not demeaning you or belittling you. When God shows you an area of your life that is an encumbrance or a hindrance, that is a powerful gift. If you're a golfer and somebody walks up and says, "I can show you a way to take four strokes off your golf game." That's not criticism. That's a gift. If somebody reviews your financial statement and says, "I can show you a way to save a thousand dollars a week." They're not condemning you. They're giving you a gift. When the Holy Spirit touches a part of your life with that kind of an invitation, it's a gift. Cooperate with Him. There's a power available to change the outcome of your life. Don't hide it. Don't deny it.

Now the alternative is condemnation, and the Holy Spirit never condemns you. Condemnation says, "You made a mistake because you are a mistake and you're always going to make a mistake and there's nothing you can do about it, so why would you try? You're a loser." The message will come in a way that you'll be tempted to receive, but the fundamental essence of it is: "You'll never change, so why would you try." The Bible says in the book of Romans that there is now no condemnation to those who are in Christ Jesus.

The question I'm asked perhaps more than any on this topic comes from the verse that talks about an unpardonable sin towards the Holy Spirit. And people will come to me with a lot of grief and anguish and say, "Pastor, I'm concerned I've done that." I'll give you the shorthand answer on it. If you're concerned about it, you haven't done it. I think at the point you make that choice, you won't care anymore. So if you still have a concern, you're good to go. Don't let the Devil condemn you.

---

3. CONSCIENCE CLEANSED

There's another way the Spirit of God helps us. He cleanses our consciences. And this is powerful. Hebrews 9:14:

How much more, then, will the blood of Christ, who through the eternal Spirit offered himself unblemished to God, cleanse our consciences from acts that lead to death, so that we may serve the living God!

HEBREWS 9:14

Our ultimate agenda in life is to serve God. The best things in life will come to you from serving Him. He will deal with the problems and elevate you above the challenges and provide the resources. God will provide everything we need for life and for godliness, if we'll serve Him.

In the scripture from Hebrews we're also told that the Spirit of God will cleanse our consciences. This verse is more meaningful with a little bit of knowledge of Scripture. Jesus, in John's Gospel, gives us a lengthy discourse about the Holy Spirit and what He'll do when He comes. One of the things He says the Holy Spirit will do is teach us what Jesus accomplished for us with His redemptive work—His death and resurrection. And here the author of Hebrews says it's through the blood of Christ that our conscience is cleansed. The Spirit will help us understand why Jesus' crucifixion and resurrection has the power to cleanse our conscience. Conversely, the Devil is an accuser. One of the titles given him in Scripture is the "accuser of the brethren," and we have all kinds of internal messages that will cripple us if we don't know how to unleash the power of the Spirit to delete those messages. Look at the last line in that verse again. It says that it will cleanse our consciences from "acts that lead to death, so that we can serve the living God." If you don't know how to have your conscience cleansed, it will limit your ability to serve the Lord.

I can give you examples from my own life. If somebody comes and they want me to pray for them because their knee hurts, I get a little message that goes off inside: "Well, who are you to pray for them to be better when your own knee hurts? You hypocrite." You may not get messages like that, but I do. Let me put it another way. Long before social media captured every image of you for time and posterity, the Devil was doing that. The Devil will remind you of your weakest moment, your greatest failure, and your greatest shortcoming. You'll have a mental image of the day you kicked the dog across three yards in full view of the children. The Devil will remind you of that at just the moment you are getting ready to say to the family, "Let's pray." You'll think, *Well, the kids don't want to pray with me; they watched me kick Fluffy right over the back fence. They have prayed about me; they don't want to pray with me.* That event may have been ten years ago, but the Devil is a master at crippling you if you don't know how to find freedom through the blood of Jesus Christ. The Devil will accuse in ways that are relentless and shameless. He's evil, and you need a power to defeat him, and it's available in the Person of the Holy Spirit. We should cooperate with Him.

Let us draw near to God with a sincere heart in full assurance of faith, having our hearts sprinkled to cleanse us from a guilty conscience and having our bodies washed with pure water.

HEBREWS 10:22

III. WALK BY THE SPIRIT

So I say, live by the Spirit, and you will not gratify the desires of the sinful nature. For the sinful nature desires what is contrary to the Spirit, and the Spirit what is contrary to the sinful nature. They are in conflict with each other, so that you do not do what you want. But if you are led by the Spirit, you are not under law. The acts of the sinful nature are obvious: sexual immorality, impurity and debauchery; idolatry and witchcraft; hatred, discord, jealousy, fits of rage, selfish ambition, dissensions, factions and envy; drunkenness, orgies, and the like. I warn you, as I did before, that those who live like this will not inherit the kingdom of God. But the fruit of the Spirit is love, joy, peace, patience, kindness, goodness, faithfulness, gentleness and self-control. Against such things there is no law. Those who belong to Christ Jesus have crucified the sinful nature with its passions and desires. Since we live by the Spirit, let us keep in step with the Spirit.

GALATIANS 5:16-25

I want to give you verse 16 of the above scripture in two different translations because they give you a subtle difference that I think is helpful. The New International Version® says, "So I say, live by the Spirit, and you will not gratify the desires of the sinful nature." But the New American Standard Bible® translation says, "I say, walk by the Spirit, and you will not carry out the desire of the flesh." The flesh is a word used in the New Testament. There are several words that share the common meaning—the flesh, your sinful nature, your Adamic nature—it's the part of us that comes from Adam. Its our carnal nature—that part that we all have even as Christ-followers, that still wants to do ungodly stuff. Did you know you have a carnal nature? If you're not aware that you have one, I bet you're probably aware that somebody you live with has one. We've all got a sinful nature, and the Bible says if we live by the Spirit we won't satisfy that part of us.

In verse 17 it says: "For the sinful nature desires what is contrary to the Spirit and the Spirit what is contrary to the sinful nature. They are in conflict with each other, so that you do not do what you want." Have you noticed that? How many times have you promised yourself you'll do better, then you walk away and you don't. There's a conflict within us.

Verse 18 says, "If you are led by the Spirit, you are not under law [as a means of righteousness]." Being led by the Spirit will lead you to a different kind of a life.

Then verse 19 says, "The acts of the sinful nature are obvious...."

In the world in which we live I don't think the acts of sinful nature are that obvious anymore because there are so many authoritative, celebrated voices that are speaking to us about ungodly things and saying they're not wrong. That's why we desperately need the counsel of Scripture. Remember we read in 1 Timothy 4 about deceiving spirits and the powerful, spiritually motivated, demonic deception they bring? We are living in it— we see it. We see things being called good now that have been called not good for a long, long time. We are deceived. In order to protect ourselves from deception we need the boundaries of Scripture. Paul gives us a list. It's not an inclusive list, but he says in verse 19 that "the acts of the sinful nature are obvious," and then he begins to list some of them: "sexual immorality, impurity, debauchery."

Let's use sexual immorality as an example. In the culture we live in today it's not obvious why sexual immorality is wrong because we hear what all of the authoritative voices speaking for it are saying. But we don't know what God said about it. It is very important to understand that God created sex, and that He created us as sexual beings. He also went to great lengths to define the context for sexual activity, because outside of the context He intended, it is destructive. He defined marriage and said sexual activity in the context of marriage is holy, pure, and undefiled.

One of the points of deception in our culture is that sexual activity is just for pleasure. We think of it as predominantly a pleasure when there is actually an assignment and a responsibility with it. God said to multiply and replenish the earth. Sexual activity without an awareness or acceptance of that assignment dissolves our responsibility to children. Think of sexual activity beyond the boundaries of marriage and the impact that has on the unborn. The result is that the we have aborted more than 60,000,000 children because they were inconvenient. They impinge on our pleasure.

God said sexual activity before you're married is not helpful. Premarital sex—the biblical word is *fornication*—He says it's wrong. You cannot practice that and participate in His Kingdom. Sexual activity beyond your marriage is adultery. He said it's wrong. You cannot practice that and participate in His Kingdom. You can be forgiven of these things, you can turn away from them, you can say, "I don't want it to define me." You can have your conscience cleansed when you repent. I'm not saying that it's never touched our lives, but we have to be willing to say it's ungodly and it's not the path that we want to walk.

I think the reason that the Church is struggling so mightily to find any authoritative voice in our current culture is because we've ignored those foundational boundaries on sexuality for decades. We've looked at things like fornication and adultery and extramarital sex with kind of a wink and a nod and said, "Ahh, you know it's not that big a deal." But it is a big deal, and I doubt there's any of us that haven't been touched by it directly or indirectly. Because of that, our consciences are a bit impaired and we need the help of the Holy Spirit to cleanse us. He will. Don't justify it—don't excuse it. Say, "God, I'm sorry. I took liberty and license, and I didn't choose to honor You. I want Your help." If we will cooperate with God and allow the power of God to cleanse us, it will give us an authority to face the challenges of our day. God's way is better.

Back to chapter 5 of Galatians—verse 22 lists the fruit of the Spirit. When you cooperate with the Spirit of God these things will grow in your life: love, joy, peace, patience, kindness, goodness, gentleness, faithfulness, and self-control. Those come by cooperating. You need the power of God to let those things emerge in you. They will not come automatically. Selfishness, greed, envy—those things will come automatically. But it says in verse 24: "Those who belong to Christ Jesus have crucified the sinful nature with its passions and desires." It's an easy sentence to read, but the idea of crucifixion is not. What do you do with your old sinful nature? The biblical prescription is to crucify it.

Folks, I've got bad news. There is no comfortable way to be crucified. I think you'd have to say that at the very best, crucifixion is uncomfortable. We're being told there's going to be an internal struggle within us and it isn't going to be easy. It's not easy following the Lord—anymore than it is easy to be an elite athlete. The benefits are worthwhile, and the effort is justified, but let's not pretend this is easy. It's only easy if it's not you. You look at your thin friend and go, "Oh, it's easy for them to be that way. They have good genes. Me, I have genes that like chocolate." We have crucified the sinful nature with its passions and desires, so let's live by the Spirit.

How do we do what Galatians 5, verse 25 says? "Since we live by the Spirit, let us keep in step with the Spirit." I've presented this verse before and apparently I've made it sound as if we were going to take a casual stroll with the Holy Spirit. A man met me afterward and he was pretty worked up. He said, "Have you ever been in the military?" I said, "No sir." And he said, "I thought so." I stood a little straighter, and he said, "Have you ever had to drill?" I said, "I don't think in the way that you mean." He said, "Well, do you know how you learn to do that?" And I said, "No sir." He said, "By hour after hour after hour after hour of practice." And then he said, "The entire group can turn at the same point and put their foot down at the same time." He said, "When you read 'keep in step with the Spirit' that's what I saw." And I said, "Thank you." Because honestly, I kind of saw me walking through the woods looking at Bambi and Thumper. I realized God had just refined my imagination for me a little bit. The Holy Spirit is your Friend. There is power available to help you. Don't treat that casually.

PRAYER: Heavenly Father, fill me with Your Spirit. Give me an understanding heart to cooperate with You. I lay aside all ungodliness that might hinder or entangle me. I forgive those who have mistreated me. Forgive me for my transgressions and willful disobedience. Cleanse me that I may walk uprightly before You. May I be clothed with power from on high to live a life that pleases You, in Jesus' name. Amen.

UNLEASHING THE POWER OF THE HOLY SPIRIT

LIFE IN THE SPIRIT

We want to welcome the Person of the Holy Spirit. If you want the power of God at work on your behalf, then by definition, you want the Person of the Holy Spirit without measure. You don't have to be afraid of Him. He won't embarrass you or humiliate you. He won't make you roll on the floor, swing on a rope, or bark like a dog. If you're doing those things it's because you like to roll, swing, and bark. Don't blame things like that on the Lord. Most of you, some of you at least, have been around places or groups of people where somebody says, "You know, I didn't want to do it, but the Lord made me or God made me or the Holy Spirit." No, He didn't. God won't violate your free will.

If He were going to violate your free will, how many of you know He should have stopped you from doing a whole lot of stuff? But He's just let us rock on with our bad selves.

So you don't have to be afraid of what the Holy Spirit will make you do. In fact, He won't come where He's not welcome. If you're not sure you want His presence in your life, relax—He's not going to bother you. He's not a party crasher. He won't come where He's not welcome.

One agenda I have is to hopefully cultivate a desire for the presence of the Person of the Holy Spirit in your life. The theme of this section is very simply, "Life in the Spirit." How do we conduct Spirit-led lives? What's that even mean for us? Should we care about it? To help answer those questions I want to begin with a collection of verses. I think it's helpful as you read your Bible to see the breadth of the presentation of the Spirit of God in Scripture. It's not like there's a singular proof text or a particular chapter or one particular author—the Spirit of God is the fabric of the story of the Bible.

In 2 Timothy chapter 1 in verse 14, Paul is writing from a Roman prison to a young man who is his protégé. He says,

Guard the good deposit that was entrusted to you--guard it with the help of the Holy Spirit who lives in us.

2 TIMOTHY 1:14

He's not talking about a bank account. He's talking about a spiritual deposit, and he says you'll be able to guard what God has given to you with the help of the Holy Spirit who is in you.

The Spirit of God, if you're a Christ-follower, lives in you and is there to help you. In fact, one of the titles Jesus attributed to the Holy Spirit is our Helper. If you want to know why you would welcome the Person of the Holy Spirit, it's so that He can help you. Isn't that good to know? When I'm at the end of myself or at the limits of my own ability—or my own wisdom or my own strength or my own knowledge—it's good to have the help of the Holy Spirit.

Look at Ephesians 4 in verse 30. It says,

> *Do not grieve the Holy Spirit of God, with whom you were*
> *sealed for the day of redemption.*
>
> EPHESIANS 4:30

This was Paul writing to the Ephesian Church, and his counsel to them is to not grieve the Holy Spirit of God. Do you live with that idea—that your choices, your life, who you are and what you do could grieve the Holy Spirit? Most of us have some formation of ideas around what's appropriate for church—the language that's appropriate for church or the clothes or behavior. But I would like to expand that a little bit because when you leave the church building or you leave the church campus, you don't leave the Holy Spirit behind. You don't pick Him up when you pull onto the property and check Him when you leave. He's in you. So if there's a joke you wouldn't tell at the altar of the church, I would suggest you probably shouldn't tell it anywhere else. Some of you just got a lot duller.

I want to expand your imagination. Live in such a way in your home, do business in such a way, recreate in such a way that you have this imagination—that you are pleasing to the Spirit of God. If you want His help, it might be a worthwhile adjustment to think, *How could I live in a way that would please Him.* Not that you earn His blessing. You don't qualify or score points, but we don't want to grieve Him.

Let me set up a passage from Psalm 51. Psalm 51 is David's great Prayer of Repentance. King David was the king of Israel, and he had committed adultery. To cover up his act of adultery, he committed murder. I mean, he wasn't on a good roll. God sent a prophet to the king's palace to say, "What you've done is not a secret." That was a very dangerous assignment for a prophet, because an ancient, Near Eastern monarch was an absolute authority. David could have had him executed as easily as he had Bathsheba's husband executed. But the prophet went nonetheless, and David knew that his sin was exposed. And to his credit, he repented. Psalm 51 is a marvelous prayer of repentance and could be used as a template. But right now I'm just going to reference one verse. In Psalm 51:11 David says,

Do not cast me from your presence or take your Holy Spirit from me.

PSALM 51:11

I want to invite you to this notion that the Spirit of God is not your right.

You know, we live in such a rights-conscious culture. I think it's because we have so much; we're so privileged. We have so much affluence and so many opportunities and such liberty and freedom. You may not have what you want, but you have more than almost anybody that's ever lived on the planet. We have derived a sense of entitlement that's just about to overwhelm us.

I don't want you to imagine that you're entitled to the Spirit of God. His presence in your life is a tremendous gift. It's a gift, and we need a little adjustment in the Church—not to presume upon Him. I want you to hear David's prayer: "Don't take Your Holy Spirit from me." What I want to cultivate in my heart and invite you to consider for your own is this desire—a longing for the presence of the Spirit of God. Not with some boundary or limit—a desire for His presence. What could I do, how could I respond, where could I stand, what prayer could I pray, that would cause the Spirit of God to come more fully upon my life? It's a good place. In fact, for all of the power, wealth and things King David had at his disposal, his primary concern when he recognized the condition of his life was, "Don't take Your Spirit from me." When the judgment of God came, David forfeited many things, but he prayed, "Don't take Your Spirit from me."

Lets go to a verse from Isaiah chapter 63. Isaiah is speaking about the Exodus generation—a group of people who had lived hundreds of years previously. He says,

> *They rebelled and grieved His Holy Spirit. So He turned and*
> *became their enemy and He himself fought against them.*

ISAIAH 63:10

They rebelled and grieved His Holy Spirit. A group of people who experienced the miraculous, the supernatural, the involvement of God in their lives—they rebelled. What did their rebellion look like? They refused to believe God; they refused to go any further. They said, "We've gone as far as we want to go. We don't want any more. We're done."

You see, I think we're pretty casual with belief. We think of belief as kind of a smorgasbord or a menu we can choose item one and seven and eleven, but we don't have to pay any attention to the rest. The opportunity to live a life in conjunction with Almighty God, empowered by the Spirit of God, is a privilege. We want to grow in belief. We want to let that emerge in our hearts. We don't want to stand back in rebellion and pride and our own self-absorption and say, "Well, you know, I don't know. I'm just not so sure." Now, if you're learning about the Lord and you're beginning, that's an appropriate beginning point, but you don't want to do that if you imagine you're growing in the Lord. I think we've rather arrogantly had this notion—you say, "Well, you know, God, what I really want to do is not go to Hell. I don't know if I really want to serve You. I'm not really too excited about being, like, an over the top Christ-follower. But in the event You're real and there is someplace else, I don't want to go someplace else. So, what's the minimum requirement?" We may not say it out loud, but we tend to approach our faith like that. I want to invite you away from that—to a life in the Spirit, a life invested in the things of God.

I. CONCEIVING OF SPIRITUAL THINGS

I want to walk through some ideas that will help us gain insight into spiritual things, to conceive of spiritual things. I think oftentimes we're kind of spiritually illiterate, or if not illiterate, just unaware or perhaps just unconcerned. They just don't matter that much to us. We haven't really attached that much significance to them, and the Bible invites us to a very different response to our lives.

A. GOD IS SPIRIT

In John chapter 4 it says,

God is spirit, and his worshipers must worship in spirit and in truth.

JOHN 4:24

God is a spirit. The first chapters of Genesis tell us that God brought order to this world. It identifies God as the Creator— the Sustainer of all things—that the spiritual gave rise to the material or the physical. So spiritual things are real. We worship something that's not carved out of stone or something in the image of an animal or a human being. That's the reason graven images were forbidden, because any image you would make of something on earth, you'd be worshipping something that the Creator made. It's backwards. Spiritual things are real. God is Spirit and we worship an Almighty God.

B. YOU ARE A SPIRIT, YOU LIVE IN A BODY, AND YOU HAVE A SOUL

Let's add to that a second idea—and it's more personal this time. It's a description of ourselves. You are a spirit, you live in a body, and you have a soul. We are complex persons. We're not just a collection of molecules. We're not just a formulation of dust from the ground. You are a spirit.

Look at Zechariah 12:

The LORD, who stretches out the heavens, who lays the

foundation of the earth, and who forms the spirit of man within him.

ZECHARIAH 12:1

In Jeremiah, it says God knows you when you're knit together in your mother's womb. He acknowledges the biological process of growth and maturing physically, but it says that God forms the spirit of man within you. Your spirit is as much a part of you as your thumbprint, created by God.

You live in a body. I like to refer to it as your earth suit, because to have spiritual authority under the sun you need an earth suit. It's why we have that incarnation story, that the Son of God became a human being—born of a woman, the Bible says. Because in order to be our Redeemer, He needed a body, so He became one of us. Seated at the right hand of God, the Father Almighty, today is the Man, Jesus Christ. It's the greatest expression of the love of God for you and me, and it's centered in the fact that He became one of us. He got one of these bodies. But when you are born, your body is born—you're born with a countdown clock. It's not eternal. Your spirit is eternal. When your body ceases to function, your spirit will not cease to function. Your body has an expiration date on it. We all do. The Bible says there are two appointments we all share: death, and after death to face judgment.

Around the front of the platform at my church they've got these big plasma screen TVs. They use them for the worship and the choir and to send me messages if I'm in real trouble. When I step to the podium they start a countdown clock. Isn't that rude? I'm really good at ignoring stuff like that. But I have a British friend—one of the finest Bible teachers I know in the world—and he was invited to the same conference. The countdown clock really, really annoyed him. I bet he referenced it a dozen times in thirty minutes. In fact, he started negotiating with them for more time from the podium. I could have told him that was not going to help.

You and I are born with a countdown clock. Your body has an expiration date, but your spirit doesn't. Your soul—your mind, your will and your emotions—they're very much a part of you. They're not a weaker part of you or an unimportant part of you. We're complex beings.

Most of us have some awareness of how to care for ourselves physically. You prepare yourself for the day each day, I hope. You know how to do that. You have some consciousness of how to take care of your emotional well-being and your mental well-being. But I'm a bit concerned because I think we have very little awareness of what spiritual health is about. We just don't give it much effort. What if you spent as much time on a daily basis with your spiritual well-being as you did with your physical well-being? Boy, that'd be a dramatic change in life, wouldn't it? And we're church folks. You are a spirit, you live in a body, and you have a soul.

I want to talk about a passage in Luke 8. Luke is a physician, you'll recall, and he writes us this little vignette. Jesus is invited to pray for a girl who's sick, and before Jesus arrives she dies. That's not good. That's poor pastoral care. But Jesus is not daunted, because He isn't intimidated by death. That's where we step into the narrative. It says,

> *Meanwhile, all the people were wailing and mourning for her. "Stop wailing," Jesus said. "She is not dead but asleep." They laughed at him, knowing that she was dead. But he took her by the hand and said, "My child, get up!"*

LUKE 8:52-54

And in verse 55, Luke makes a very unique observation. He says,

> *Her spirit returned...*

LUKE 8:55

The implication is clear: Her spirit had departed. You see, physical death—when your body ceases to function—is not the end of your existence. You've heard of Leonardo da Vinci, the

Renaissance Man—great artist, great scientist, thinker, student— it's reported that he conducted a number of experiments with people that were at the point of death. He would put them on a scale to see if there was a discernible change in their body weight when their spirit departed. And we think we're so smart. You are a spirit, you live in a body, and you have a soul.

C. BORN OF THE SPIRIT

The Bible talks to us about being born of the Spirit. In the same way that you have a physical birth, the Bible says that you can have a spiritual birth. It's an interesting notion, and Jesus talked about it in John chapter 3 when Nicodemus comes to see him. Nicodemus is a leader amongst the religious Jewish community, who are God's chosen people. But he still wants to talk to Jesus because he recognizes Jesus' unique authority and power. He's a little afraid of the opinions of the others, so he comes at night, in a covert way to see Jesus. The point of the discussion becomes— how do you participate in the Kingdom of God. And we're going to step into the middle of the narrative.

In reply Jesus declared, "I tell you the truth, no one can see the kingdom of God unless he is born again. ... Flesh gives birth to flesh, but the Spirit gives birth to spirit. You should not be surprised at my saying, 'You must be born again.' The wind blows wherever it pleases. You hear its sound, but you cannot

tell where it comes from or where it is going. So it is with
everyone born of the Spirit."

JOHN 3:3,6-8

This verse says, "No one can see the kingdom of God unless
he is born again." The "no one" carries a special significance
here because it's saying Nicodemus, who's not only a Jew but
a leader in the Jewish community, cannot see the Kingdom
of God without being born again. And then Jesus goes on to
amplify. He says, "Flesh gives birth to flesh, but the Spirit gives
birth to spirit." There's a correlation between a physical birth
and a spiritual birth. "You should not be surprised at my saying,
'You must be born again.' The wind blows wherever it pleases.
You hear its sound, but you cannot tell where it comes from or
where it is going. So it is with everyone born of the Spirit." It's
an interesting parallel. Jesus says, "The wind—you don't know its
origin, and you're not sure about it and you can't control it. But
you can certainly experience its impact. You can benefit from it."
He says, "So is the Holy Spirit. You don't know fully where He's
coming from, and you don't control Him. You certainly don't
manipulate the Holy Spirit. Don't try. But you can benefit from
His impact—from His presence." And He uses the context to
describe this spiritual birth. To be a participant in the Kingdom
of God, you have to be birthed into it. You don't become a
Christ-follower by joining a church. You don't become a Christ-
follower because you get an appropriate doctrine or theological

statement or by a moral position or an ethical creed. To be a Christ-follower isn't joining a group. There's really good news in that. If joining a group, a particular denomination, or tradition made you a Christ-follower, then they would have the ability to keep you out. The birth into the Kingdom of God is a very personal decision. The Bible says it's available to every human being—that no one is excluded, that God has made a revelation of Himself to every person—that any person can choose to be birthed into the Kingdom of God. It says it takes place by a decision you make about a Person. His name is Jesus—specifically, Jesus of Nazareth.

There were, no doubt, many people named Jesus in the first century—the one we're referencing grew up in a little village in the northern part of Israel called Nazareth. Jesus of Nazareth, we're told, was the Christ, the Messiah, the Anointed One, the Son of God. You can believe those things and not experience a spiritual birth, because at that point it's just an historical acknowledgment. It's a statement. But you can take a step beyond that and say, "I believe Jesus of Nazareth is the Christ, and I would accept Him as Lord of my life." In essence what you're saying is, "God, I'm a sinner, and I need help. I can't save myself. I can't be good enough or kind enough or moral enough or generous enough or anything else enough. I need help. Forgive me of my sins." That's what the Jesus-story is about. He took the price that I deserved for my rebellion and my godlessness so that I could have all the benefits through His perfect righteousness.

When you choose Jesus as Lord, that's about priority. If He's Lord, He gets to call the cadence of your life. That's why Jesus taught us to pray: "Not my will, but Your will be done." You see, Jesus being Lord of your life means that the priorities for your life are established by our Lord, and then we serve Him as King. The Bible says if you're willing to do that, you can be birthed into the Kingdom of God. Isn't that magnificent? Nobody can keep you out if you want to be a participant.

I think one of the great limits that we've had in American Christendom (and I've been a part of that most of my life, so I'm not throwing a stone) is we tend to stop the discussion at that point. The emphasis tends to be on how to be birthed into the Kingdom of God, so we talk to people about, "Have you said the Sinner's Prayer? Have you made a profession of faith?" Maybe, "Have you been dunked in the tank?" And that's important, so if you haven't been, get in the line. But we kind of stop the discussion at that point. Folks, that's not the objective. When we go to the hospital to see newborns and we celebrate the life, the real celebration is about the potential that life represents—the future that comes with maturing and the developmental skills and the emerging personality and the gifts that will be resident there and all that life's going to afford—that's why we celebrate. Truth be told, when you first get here you're just kind of a hot mess, right? You just make noise and odors and consume stuff. At that point, we're waiting for the payoff.

But in a similar way we're birthed into the Kingdom of God to grow up, and we need the help of the Holy Spirit to do that. We have to have the desire. Have you heard the phrase, "the Bride of Christ?" The Bible talks about the Church being the Bride of Christ—that Jesus is coming back for a "bride without spot or wrinkle." Folks, I think you know intuitively that we don't offer babies as brides. By definition to be a bride you've got to at least reach some point of maturity. We've got to grow up in the Lord. And what that looks like is that we have a desire, interest, and care that the character of God be formed in us. It means our desire for the things of God is increasing and growing—that our awareness of spiritual things would be escalating and multiplying. It means God's will and His interest in the earth is more important to us. That means we're growing up, spiritually. You say, "Well, wait a minute, I just thought I was supposed to come to church when I could, because I didn't want to go to Hell." May I make a suggestion? If the things of God don't really matter all that much to you and you know you don't really do the things you need to do—don't pretend. Tell the Lord the truth. I don't mean that to scold you, and I certainly don't want you to feel ashamed. I have worked this out in my own life. I've had to learn to be honest with the Lord. There's some pressure in the midst of a religious gathering to go along to get along, and I'm not even sure that's evil. But don't let that define your relationship with the Lord. Tell the Lord the truth. If you don't care that much about the things of the Lord, tell Him. Say, "God, You know, I probably think You're real, but I've been a whole lot more interested in my way than Yours. Help me." Now here's what I've discovered: He will.

You'll have to walk the path. I can give you an example from my own life. I grew up, predominantly, in a Christian home, and so I knew from pretty early on I was supposed to like reading my Bible. So when I got old enough to make my own decision, I would try to read my Bible, and it was awful. I like to read. I mean, back before it was electronic and digital, I've always liked it. So I thought, *Well, if I can read all these other books. I can read my Bible.* I'd get my Bible out, and suddenly I'd be drowsy; I'd go to sleep! I mean, I could read other books all day long and not feel tired at all. Then I'd get that Bible out and suddenly exhaustion would come over me. So finally I said to the Lord, "You know, God, I know You've sold a lot of copies, but I'm reasonably well read, and Your book's a little dry. Nothing personal, mind You, but I need some help." He didn't strike me. And it didn't happen in a day or even in a week, but I can tell you over time it has become the most precious book I've ever read. I mean, I know I'm in church and I'm a pastor and I'm supposed to say that, but truthfully, it is the most interesting book I've ever picked up. It fascinates me. I know God did that. I didn't do that. So don't pretend. Tell Him the truth. Say, "God, I'm struggling with this, but I would like to grow up." You see, I don't think you want to show up at the Pearly Gates in Pampers™ with a silver rattle. When you see St. Peter, you don't want to have to take your paci out to greet him. I promise. You don't want to meet the Prophet Elijah wearing a onesie with a paci clipped to it. He will laugh at you. I know him that well from Scripture. Okay?

D. YOUR SPIRIT IS ETERNAL

Now your spirit is eternal—we've already touched on that but lets look at this scripture:

> *There was a rich man who was dressed in purple and fine linen and lived in luxury every day. At his gate was laid a beggar named Lazarus, covered with sores and longing to eat what fell from the rich man's table. Even the dogs came and licked his sores. "The time came when the beggar died and the angels carried him to Abraham's side. The rich man also died and was buried. In hell, where he was in torment, he looked up and saw Abraham far away, with Lazarus by his side. So he called to him, "Father Abraham, have pity on me and send Lazarus to dip the tip of his finger in water and cool my tongue, because I am in agony in this fire."*
>
> LUKE 16:19-24

Now look at John 12. I like this passage a lot. Jesus is speaking to a group of Jewish leaders in Jerusalem. It's first century, and He says,

> *For this reason they could not believe, because, Isaiah says elsewhere: "He has blinded their eyes and deadened their*

hearts, so they can neither see with their eyes, nor understand
with their hearts, nor turn--and I would heal them." Isaiah
said this because he saw Jesus' glory and spoke about him.

JOHN 12:39-41

I like how verse 41 gives us a little insight into Isaiah when it
says, "He saw Jesus' glory." If you're just reading this casually and
you're not aware of the timeline of the Bible you'd think, *Well,*
Isaiah was probably a contemporary of Jesus. You would maybe
think that Isaiah hung out in Galilee and fished with Peter
and James and John. But he didn't. Isaiah was a court prophet
in Jerusalem during the time of the nation of Judah, some five
hundred years before Jesus. And yet it says that Isaiah "saw Jesus'
glory and spoke about him." How could you do that? You know
he's not like Methuselah, Jr. He didn't live to be five hundred
years old. He saw something spiritually.

Since your spirit is eternal, it has insight and understanding and
awareness that's not limited to time. In the Gospels, Jesus was
constantly talking to us about this tension between time and
eternity. He didn't want us to be limited in our perspective by
our awareness of time. He would say things like, "Don't just lay
up treasure on earth, but layup treasure in Heaven." He's not
against affluence, but He was saying, it's far better to lay up
treasure in Heaven, because in Heaven it won't be diminished.
In Heaven it's not subject to a market crash or corruption or
rust—whatever treasure you lay up in Heaven has eternal value

and is a better investment. You have a limited run under the sun. Remember the countdown clock? Use your days under the sun to lay up treasure in Heaven. He talked to us about being wise stewards and leveraging the opportunity of our days.

The tension between time and eternity fills our lives. It fills the pages of the Bible. Remember when Jesus stood before Pilate, the Roman governor? Pilate thought he was interviewing Him because he could either condemn Him to death by crucifixion or he could set Him free. He was asking Jesus questions and not getting much response. Jesus was being kind of quiet, and finally Pilate said, "Do you know who I am?" It's kind of funny if you think about it—the Roman governor standing before the Son of God. To be a Roman governor was pretty impressive credentials. I mean, after all, he has the authority of the Roman Senate behind him and the Roman Legions at hand. He had the capability to inflict a lot of things, and he does ultimately order Jesus' execution. But he got all puffed up and said, "Do you know who I am?!" Every time I read that I wish Jesus had said, "Well, as a matter of fact…" You know Pilate will see Jesus again. Except the next time, Jesus will be sitting on the throne. Do you think Jesus will look at Pilate and say, "Do you know who I Am?" I digress. Jesus did answer him by basically saying, "The only power you have—and you do have some power—but the only power you have my Dad gave you." That would have been a good point to hit rewind.

As you and I live in this tension between time and eternity, part of our spiritual awareness is our investment in eternity. Don't miss it. The Holy Spirit will help you see where you are storing up treasure. That's why Jesus told us He would be our Helper.

E. SPIRITUAL OPPRESSION

Let me take a couple of minutes with one more piece of this that I'm calling "Spiritual Oppression." We could call it spiritual conflict. There are a lot of labels, but the reality is there is a tension spiritually in our world. The will of God is not fully in play in our world. If it were, Jesus wouldn't have taught us to pray the way He did. He said, "Pray this way. Our Father who is in Heaven, hallowed be Your Name. Your Kingdom come, Your will be done, on earth as it is in Heaven." If God's will were fully enforced in the earth, Jesus wouldn't have asked us to pray for that. With just a casual glance at our world and the history of humanity and civilization, it's very apparent that we do some heinous things in this world. Evil exists. There's a conflict between good and evil. So when you become a Christ-follower, by virtue of your birth into the Kingdom of God and your participation in the Kingdom of God, you inherit an adversary. You might say, "I don't like that." Well, I appreciate that you don't like it, but it doesn't change the facts.

If you're a U.S. citizen, there are people in the world

that don't like you. You don't have to be mean spirited. You don't have to be hateful or intolerant or ugly. They simply don't like you by virtue of your nationality and your citizenship. If you haven't traveled broadly enough to know that yet, I assure you it's true. They would do you harm just because of your citizenship. Being polite will not change their mind, in the same way that being polite spiritually will not change the mind of evil.

The only thing that evil will yield to is a power greater than itself. It's true in the physical world, and it's true in the spiritual world. That means awareness of spiritual things—good and evil—is helpful if you're going to thrive spiritually, physically, or any other way.

I want you to take a look at Mark chapter 9, verses 17-29. It says,

> *A man in the crowd answered, "Teacher, I brought you my son, who is possessed by a spirit that has robbed him of speech. Whenever it seizes him, it throws him to the ground. He foams at the mouth, gnashes his teeth and becomes rigid. I asked your disciples to drive out the spirit, but they could not." "O unbelieving generation," Jesus replied, "how long shall I stay with you? How long shall I put up with you? Bring the boy to me." So they brought him. When the spirit saw Jesus,*

it immediately threw the boy into a convulsion. He fell to the ground and rolled around, foaming at the mouth. Jesus asked the boy's father, "How long has he been like this?" "From childhood," he answered. "It has often thrown him into fire or water to kill him. But if you can do anything, take pity on us and help us." "'If you can'?" said Jesus. "Everything is possible for him who believes." Immediately the boy's father exclaimed, "I do believe; help me overcome my unbelief!" When Jesus saw that a crowd was running to the scene, he rebuked the evil spirit. "You deaf and mute spirit," he said, "I command you, come out of him and never enter him again." The spirit shrieked, convulsed him violently and came out. The boy looked so much like a corpse that many said, "He's dead." But Jesus took him by the hand and lifted him to his feet, and he stood up. After Jesus had gone indoors, his disciples asked him privately, "Why couldn't we drive it out?" He replied, "This kind can come out only by prayer."

MARK 9:17-29

It sounds like the boy was having some type of seizure-like activity, doesn't it? Except we're invited into the insight that there's a spiritual component to it. Do I think that every seizure-like activity has a demonic motivation? No, the Bible doesn't say that. But this passage seems to suggest that at least in this instance it did. Today, Christians respond to the idea of this in some unusual ways. You say, "Well, I don't believe that."

You certainly have the right to believe whatever you want to. God's given us a free will. But not believing it doesn't make it not true or remove you from its influence. It'd be like standing in the middle of a busy interstate and saying, "I don't believe in cars." It would not make it a safer place to stand. So be sure that your belief is informed by a truth greater than just your life-experience. In verse 19 Jesus says, "Oh unbelieving generation, how long shall I stay with you? How long shall I put up with you? Bring the boy to me." Who's He talking to? He's talking to His disciples—they've tried to help the father and his son and they were unable, and Jesus basically said, "You know, aren't you guys paying any attention at all? Bring the boy to Me." In verse 20, the boy immediately began to convulse when they brought him to Jesus. The dark spirit began to convulse within the boy because it had an insight into who Jesus was that most people didn't. Spiritual forces have some awareness about spiritual things that you and I don't. This is not a comfortable scene. There's very little about this that's pleasant. There's a young man who's very ill and a father who's very desperate. He's at the end of his options. You know that, or he would not have come to a public place and brought his son who was so troubled, to put him in that public place for the embarrassment and all that goes with that. He'd asked the disciples for help. They couldn't help him. Then he was desperate enough that when he saw Jesus he cried out to Him and said, "Can't You help me?" It's an awkward scene. If you were in this encounter, or you met someone in this way—it would not be a comfortable place to be standing. Finally in verse 22, the father, in desperation, says to Jesus, "If you can do anything, just help me." And Jesus answers, "If you can?"

The author of the text doesn't give us any insight, but in my mind Jesus has a little bit of a wry smile. Almost like, "If I can?...Would you like me to part a sea?...If I can?" I digress...

Then Jesus gives him a key that's helpful to all of us. He says, "Everything is possible for him who believes." You see, what you choose to believe really does make a difference. If you don't believe Jesus is the Son of God, you forfeit the benefit that comes with that. Believing is that important. The father loved his son and in desperation exclaimed, "I do believe..." Almost like saying, "If believing is the key, I believe!" That's not a rational response. That's an emotive response—"If believing will help my boy, I'm a believer."

At this point in the scripture you can almost hear his brain engage. "Well, wait a minute. What if there's a test? What if He's going to ask me a question? What if there's some requirement?" And he said, "I do believe, but you better help me overcome my unbelief!" If there was a window anywhere, this father would have climbed through it in his desperation to help his son. Desperate places are not bad but they're also not comfortable or fun. I don't volunteer for them. But if you're in a desperate place today, the Lord is close to you. Notice that there was no rebuke of this father. There was no condemnation. There was no scolding. There's an invitation, there's help coming and a power available to you in the Holy Spirit to overcome.

I want to circle back on a couple of things. There was a spirit that impacted the speech of this child and caused him physical torment. The Bible doesn't say that every physical challenge and every physical problem has a spiritual origin, but it does seem to suggest that some do. You say, "I don't believe that." And you're entitled, but the Bible says it and Jesus believed that, and I'm still of the opinion that Jesus is smarter than me and probably you.

There's another lesson we can take from that passage, and that's faith in God is required. We're going to have to learn to trust the Lord. We're going to grow up in our belief. We're going to grow up in our faith.

I like to learn, so I like to be around people and observe their expertise. Recently we had a large children's event at the church. We had the church kitchen filled with people. They fed the kids multiple times every day. There was one place on campus where they were cooking all the proteins. They were smoking pork and smoking turkeys, and I was fascinated by the mountain of food that the kids went through. One day I went over and watched the guys smoking the pork. They opened this huge smoker and there were racks filled with pork, and my friend reached in and he poked it with his finger. I watched him poke about three times, and finally I said, "Why are you doing that?" And he said, "Well, I'm seeing if it's done." Folks, if I poke something in the oven all I get is a burned finger. I don't have the expertise. I don't have that training. But as the people of God, you represent this amazing collection of gifts and abilities that you've honed and cultivated. Let's cultivate some spiritual things. Let's grow up in the Lord a little bit. Invest time, energy, and resources and have the desire to grow in belief. It has value in time and for all eternity.

The previous verses in Mark chapter 9 also helped us see that spirits can come and go. Because in verse 25 when Jesus spoke to the spirit, He said, "You come out of him, and don't you ever enter him again." He closed that door. I don't believe Jesus used extraneous words. In the 29th verse, He gave us another little insight into the levels of authority in the spiritual realm. Because when the disciples asked, "Why couldn't we achieve that objective? We've had some success previously." And Jesus said, "Well that kind only comes out through prayer," basically telling them that one was a little stronger than what they'd wrestled with before. We can grow up in our faith, and the Holy Spirit will help us because He is our Helper and we desperately need Him. Say, "Holy Spirit, You are welcome in my life."

There's such comfort in knowing the Lord wants to help us. Jesus said, "I won't leave you as orphans. I won't leave you alone." That is so, so powerful in our lives.

PRAYER: Heavenly Father, You are my Strength and my Redeemer. In You I have life and hope. You watch over my days and provide for all my needs. I stand in Your faithfulness and mercy. Today I rejoice in the majesty of my God. Let all the earth resonate with the praises of Almighty God. Let the name of Jesus be lifted high—in His name I pray. Amen.

LIFE IN THE SPIRIT
PART II

Unleashing the power of the Holy Spirit is necessary. I don't know if it's apparent to you yet or not, but there is not a season coming—the season is upon us—where the only way we will flourish and the only way we will stand is through the power of the Spirit of God. It is a new day, and the implications of that will become increasingly clear with every passing week. I don't lament that. I think we are closer to the return of the Lord than we have ever been. There's not some point in time I want to go back to. You know, I don't want to go back to pre-electricity, or to my horse and buggy, or back to *Leave it to Beaver*. I'm quite content that we are in the right day and the right time with the right equipment and the Word of God and the Spirit of God within us. But I'm equally certain that we will not thrive, and we will not complete our assignment without the help of the Holy Spirit. So, I want to continue to put the invitation before you to say, "You are welcomed in my life"—to take down your preconditions, to lay aside the inhibitions you may have held—

to accept the Word of God in simplicity so that the power of God can fill your life. The premise is very simple. I've said it over and over again. From the opening chapters of the Bible to the concluding chapters of Revelation, the Spirit of God and the power of God go together. And if you are going to live in the Power of God, you're going to have to be familiar and comfortable with the Spirit of God. You can't reject the Holy Spirit. You can't diminish His place in your life. You cannot refuse to cooperate with Him, and imagine the power of God will consistently be present in your life. We will not out-think evil. We will not out-organize the demonic kingdom. We need the power of God. I'm not opposed to organization or learning or planning, but we need the power of God.

How do we live in the Spirit? Galatians gives us some lengthy counsel, and I just want to tag it, because it really is the bridge from the previous chapter:

> *For the sinful nature desires what is contrary to the Spirit, and the Spirit what is contrary to the sinful nature. They are in conflict with each other, so that you do not do what you want. But if you are led by the Spirit, you are not under law.*
>
> GALATIANS 5:17-18

I think it's worth noting, this is written to Christ-followers, not to the ungodly or the immoral. Paul is still prompting them, reminding them, nudging them, urging them to live by the Spirit. The alternative is to gratify the desires of the sinful nature. Your carnal, earthly, Adamic, sinful nature churns out all sorts of desires that are rooted in that nature. Part of growing up in the Lord is to learn to say no to them. The biblical prescription for dealing with your carnal, sinful, earthly, Adamic nature is crucifixion. We need the help of the Spirit of God to do that, because crucifixion at its very best is uncomfortable. If we had to describe crucifixion, the kindest description we could use is calling it a little uncomfortable. We should expect it to be uncomfortable when we're crucifying our old nature.

We don't earn our way to the goodness of God and the mercy or grace of God. To be led by the Spirit is to walk in the fullness of the redemptive purposes of God—to overcome that old carnal nature. Increasingly, there needs to be a distinction between the people of God and the people that are not—not in being weird or goofy or bizarre, but in what we give ourselves to and the desires of our heart. If you work or live amongst people who are not Christ-followers, there needs to be distinctiveness in your life. The desires and aspirations of your life, the dreams for your children, what you hope that they aspire to and what they become—it needs to be distinct and separate from the people who don't have the awakening of the Spirit of God within them. You have to guard your heart. There is enormous pressure of messaging that bombards us to be in the world and to be of the world. The challenge of being a Christ-follower is to be in the world but not of it. It's the old expression we've used many times: "A ship in the sea is a good thing, but the sea in the ship is not so good." So the Church in the world is a good thing, but the world in the Church is not a good thing. Being in the world on behalf of Christ is a good thing, but the world being in you will diminish Christ in you. You have to guard your heart. You have to be willing to be a little "foolish" for Jesus. It's time. If not now, when? When will we find that courage?

Here's another verse in Galatians I want to reference:

> *Do not be deceived: God cannot be mocked. A man reaps what he sows. The one who sows to please his sinful nature, from that nature will reap destruction; the one who sows to please the Spirit, from the Spirit will reap eternal life. Let us not become weary in doing good, for at the proper time we will reap a harvest if we do not give up. Therefore, as we have opportunity, let us do good to all people, especially to those who belong to the family of believers.*

GALATIANS 6:7-10

In the larger context of the book of Galatians, Paul is pleading with them. He basically says, "Who has bewitched you? You were doing really well. You had such momentum, and somebody cut in on you and you lost all your momentum." He is encouraging them back to this life in the Spirit. In verse 9, he acknowledges that they'd become weary in doing good and tries to encourage them to not give up. It makes me smile when

I read that. You know, he doesn't have to warn us to not become weary in doing wrong. Why is that? It's because we don't get tired of being selfish. We never exhaust that part of our nature. But we do grow weary in doing good. He then reminds them of the harvest that's in store IF they don't give up. You should circle that little preposition, "if." It's not automatic. It's not your right. If you give up, you forfeit your harvest. I think it's worth noting that verse 10 is a statement asking us to cooperate in response. It says, "Let us do good to all people, especially to those who belong to the family of believers."

So living life in the Spirit has to do with every facet of our lives. It's not just a particular way to pray. It's not just a particular attitude towards the supernatural. It has to do with who you are 24/7. You can't compartmentalize your life and say, "This part is for God, and this part is for business, and this part is for pleasure, or this is my private life, and this is my public life." You are going to welcome the Spirit of God into the breadth of your life. We're Christ-followers 24/7.

I. TWO PRIMARY CHOICES: BE AN OVERCOMER, OR BE OVERCOME

Romans 12:21 probably gives it to us as succinctly as any verse. It says,

Do not be overcome by evil, but overcome evil with good.

ROMANS 12:21

163

We have two options: We are either going to overcome evil, or will be overcome by evil—but to live an overcoming life, we need the help of the Spirit of God. I'm going to say it over and over and over, because I don't have a better answer. We can't join a group that makes us overcomers. We can't move to a particular street that makes us an overcomer. There is not a particular part of the nation. I've been talking to Christian leaders in cities across the nation, and they'll say to me things like, "Well, where you live everybody is a Christian." And I think, "You really need to visit where I live more." I mean, I know we're blessed, but it's too easy to decide that the reason things are the way they are is because of our location. It's not about where you live. It's about who you are and the light in you. If God's put you in an office where there aren't any Christians, there's a reason He's put you there—they needed a Christian. If you leave, what are you doing, taking the last Bible with you on the way out the door? It's important. We're going to be overcomers, or we're going to be overcome.

The book of Revelation opens with these letters to seven churches in Asia Minor, and in every case, they're challenged to overcome. It is the subplot in this larger story of the book of Revelation. How do you get to the triumphant return of the King and the New Jerusalem and the coming of the Kingdom of God to the earth? It's by being an overcomer. Early in Revelation it says,

"He who has an ear, let him hear what the Spirit says to the
churches. To him who overcomes, I will give the right to eat
from the tree of life, which is in the paradise of God"

<u>REVELATIONS 2:7</u>

You see, the right to eat from the tree of life in God's paradise
is given to the one who overcomes. And then the conclusion of
Revelation says,

He said to me: "It is done. I am the Alpha and the Omega,
the Beginning and the End. To him who is thirsty I will give
to drink without cost from the spring of the water of life. He
who overcomes will inherit all this, and I will be his God
and he will be my son. But the cowardly, the unbelieving, the
vile, the murderers, the sexually immoral, those who practice
magic arts, the idolaters and all liars--their place will be in
the fiery lake of burning sulfur. This is the second death."

<u>REVELATION 21:6-8</u>

This idea is both the opening scenario, and it's the concluding
promise—that the Kingdom of God is given to the one who
overcomes. By definition, overcoming presupposes hurdles,
obstacles, challenges, interruptions, disappointments—all
that stuff we want somebody else to have. We don't have to
overcome dessert. We have to overcome the temptation for three
desserts…that's another discussion. But let it be on the radar of

your heart that you are either overcoming on a daily basis or you being overcome. There is not a neutral. You're either overcoming in the arena of influence God has given you—you're using your ability, your skills, your resources, your strength to be an overcomer—or you're capitulating.

A triumphant Church is composed of overcoming people, not better preaching. A triumphant Church is filled with triumphant people. A growing church is filled with growing people. I'm always a bit amused at folks who say, "You know, I didn't want to be a part of a growing church." Really? A growing church is filled with growing people. A stagnant church is filled with, guess what? In which of those two churches do you want to worship? We get some goofy ideas in our heads. God has called you for something. You say, "Well, it's harder than I wish." I know. When you're a child, it's not hard. When you need something, Mom will get it. She'll just write a check. Kids do not have the concept that the check is attached to an account with a balance that has to have a deposit. "Just write one! Use your card! I want it. Mama, make it happen!" That's not an evil child. It's a child's perspective. But when you grow up, you start accepting responsibility for the balance in the account. What a hassle that is! But growing up in the Lord means your posture in the world is different.

A. IN THE ARENA

2 Timothy 4—I think Paul lives this out for us in such a beautiful way. Paul's in a Roman prison awaiting trial. He's already been tried once. He narrowly escaped condemnation to death. He seems to be anticipating that condemnation this time, and he writes this note to Timothy, a young man whom he has been mentoring. Timothy's in another city, and Paul gives his circumstances. I just think his circumstances are noteworthy. I would argue that Paul was a relatively effective advocate for Jesus of Nazareth. How many of you, when you get to Heaven, would be willing to get a reward equal to Paul's? Probably all of us. So it's not like we're talking about a slacker or somebody that wasn't invested, but I want you to note his circumstances as we go into this scripture. Paul writes to Timothy:

Do your best to come to me quickly, for Demas, because he loved this world, has deserted me and has gone to Thessalonica. Crescens has gone to Galatia, and Titus to Dalmatia. Only Luke is with me. Get Mark and bring him with you, because he is helpful to me in my ministry. I sent Tychism to Ephesus. When you come, bring the cloak that I left with Carpus at Troas, and my scrolls, especially the parchments. Alexander the metalworker did me a great deal of harm. The Lord will repay him for what he has done. You too should be on your guard against him, because he strongly opposed our message. At my first defense, no one came to my support, but everyone deserted me. May it not be held against them. But the Lord stood at my side and gave me strength, so that through me the message might be fully proclaimed and all the Gentiles might hear it. And I was delivered from the lion's mouth. The Lord will rescue me from every evil attack and will bring me safely to his heavenly kingdom. To him be glory for ever and ever. Amen.

2 TIMOTHY 4:9-18

It's easy to read through that in a hurry, but if you can, put yourself in that place. Paul is in a Roman prison. It's a miserable place. I've seen the place, and at least by tradition they say it was damp and cold—unpleasant in every way. He says to Timothy, "Could you hurry? I'm alone." And then he tells where everybody's gone. He said, "Well, Luke is with me, but Timothy, hurry. I'm cold. Could you bring me a coat?" I don't know the circumstances or why Luke couldn't address that, but he doesn't seem to be able to. "Bring me a coat, Timothy, and could you bring my parchments?" I mean, it's not a triumphant letter at the beginning.

Then he says, a metalworker named Alexander did him a great deal of harm and warns Timothy to be on guard against him, because he strongly apposed their message of Christ. This is the same Paul who spoke in Jesus' name and drove the spirit of divination out of a slave girl who was harassing them in the market place. This is the Paul that prayed for the dead, and they were raised to life again. This is Paul who, while on board a ship to Rome, when all the sailors thought they were going to drown, said, "Listen, last night, an angel of God, whose I am and whom I serve, stood before me, and we're all good to go." This is that same triumphant Paul saying to Timothy, "You need to be careful, because Alexander is powerful, and he was a strong adversary, and I suspect he'll oppose you as well." Can you hold all of that intention in your life—the power of God, the triumph of God, the victory of God, and the challenges of living in this world? I would rather wipe away part of that equation and say, "If you know the power, triumph, and victory of God then your opposition should just diminish and crumble beneath the sound of your voice." But that doesn't seem to be the story of Scripture.

Then Paul tells how no one came to his defense, but deserted him. He tells Timothy not to hold it against them. He was still confident, with the Lord remaining at his side, that the message of Christ would still be proclaimed to all the Gentiles through him.

You've got to love that about Paul. He's totally deserted in a Roman prison and said, "But it's alright because the message through me is going to be proclaimed, and I pray that all the Gentiles hear." Now that's a big vision. I'm a little embarrassed of the smallness of our vision—how we apologize for what's in our heart for the Kingdom of God. How have we been reduced down to such a narrow imagination of what God has called us to? We want the power of Almighty God at work on our behalf so our kids can get on another ball team? We need to let the Lord lift our vision a little bit. You say, "Well, I thought when my life got easy and all the problems drained away and all the challenges went away, then God would get first place in my life." No! Where did you get that? Not from the Bible.

We've talked about the tension in our lives between time and eternity. A big part of our motivation to think eternally is that our full story's not being written in time. When Paul says in verse 18, "The Lord will rescue me from every evil attack and... bring me safely to his heavenly kingdom," he's not oblivious to time—his hope is in eternity. You honor the Lord in time, and there'll be a reward in eternity you can't imagine. You see, I think one of the great joys is that Jesus is awaiting us. We will get to see Him in His glory. The last time He was on display in the world, it was on a Roman cross on a hill outside of Jerusalem. A handful of people saw Him as a resurrected Lord. But from the world's standpoint, the last public presentation of Jesus was as a crucified, condemned person by the Romans. But He's coming back with the angels in all of His glory! And you and I want to be invested in that. You want some of that in your portfolio. You do. Holy Spirit, help us.

II. AN ASSERTIVE POSTURE

I wanted to put together a list of times the people of God are encouraged to assert themselves in order to overcome. I really wanted them from a diverse set of books in the New Testament. I wanted you to see again, that this isn't a subtle theme. This isn't some isolated principle. This notion is not only the fabric of our Bible, but the assertive posture of the people of God.

In Colossians 4, it says,

> *Epaphras, who is one of you and a servant of Christ Jesus, sends greetings. He is always wrestling in prayer for you, that you may stand firm in all the will of God...*
>
> COLOSSIANS 4:12

It's interesting to me that Epaphras is "wrestling in prayer." That's as demanding as any physical activity you can engage in. Wrestling—it's harder than running. It's harder than lifting weights. It more difficult than playing basketball. He's wrestling in prayer, and the outcome—the objective for which he's wrestling—is that you may be able to "stand firm in the will of God." Apparently, it's not easy to stand firm in the will of God. In fact, we probably won't do it unless somebody's wrestling in prayer on our behalf. We are overcomers or we are overcome. Don't be surprised, the Bible says, at the trials you find yourselves in, because our brothers and sisters throughout the world are undergoing similar trials. I'm always surprised, aren't you? When it doesn't go my way, I go, "Ah, wow. How could this be?"

Look at Romans 15:

I urge you, brothers, by our Lord Jesus Christ and by the love of the Spirit, to join me in my struggle by praying to God for me.

ROMANS 15:30

He's describing his journey as a "struggle."

Look at this next verse in Ephesians:

For our struggle is not against flesh and blood, but against the rulers, against the authorities, against the powers of this dark world and against the spiritual forces of evil in the heavenly realms.

EPHESIANS 6:12

I meet so many Christ-followers—churched folks—who say, "Ahh, that's just not my deal." There's no such thing. You've just simply said, "I have yielded the field. I've chosen not to engage, therefore, I have been overcome, and I have yielded anyone under my sphere of influence." Not a prudent choice. We're being told so that we can engage in the wrestling match.

Look at 1 Timothy 6, verse 12:

Fight the good fight of the faith. Take hold of the eternal life
to which you were called when you made your good confession
in the presence of many witnesses

1 TIMOTHY 6:12

You know, I grew up around animals—horses, especially. I was always intrigued at how the animal knows innately who has the authority. You know, if the horse doesn't frighten you, it's amazing how cooperative the horse will be with your suggestions. If you're afraid of the horse, it's amazing how uncooperative the same animal will be. They know who's in charge. How do they know? I don't know. I'm not a horse psychologist. But when I read that verse in Timothy, and it says, "Take hold of eternal life," you need to know the authority you have. You need to know the Spirit of God within you. You need to know what the Word of God says belongs to you, or we will not stand. We will not take hold of what is ours. We have capitulated for too long. We have yielded the field. We've been waiting for an elected official to stand up or God to rise up—but He's called us!

The weapons we fight with are not the weapons of the
world. On the contrary, they have divine power to demolish
strongholds.

2 CORINTHIANS 10:4

It doesn't say we're not in a battle. It doesn't say we don't fight.

It just says that the tools we have are not the tools that we use secularly, or in the carnal self. We're leading a Spirit-led life. Our tools have divine power to demolish strongholds. There's that power again. If you don't take up the tools that God gives you, then you don't have divine power.

1 Corinthians 9, verse 24 says:

> *Don't you know that in a race all the runners run, but only one gets the prize? Run in such a way as to get the prize.*
>
> 1 CORINTHIANS 9:24

This is contrary to today's world where everybody gets a prize. We don't want to damage anybody's little self-image. So if you're going to run, we're going to cheer for you. It's kind of affirming when you're doing it, but it doesn't really prepare you for life, because everybody doesn't get the same outcome. Everybody doesn't have the same gift. Everybody can't run at the same pace. I mean, if you can't run at the same pace as the better runner, you've got another gift. So don't kick and scream because you can't outrun that person. Understand the gifts God has given you, and make the most of that gift. Just think about what that verse says—"Run in such a way as to get the prize." You better find the race God's called you to, and run.

Further in 1 Corinthians, Paul says:

Therefore I do not run like a man running aimlessly; I do not fight like a man beating the air. No, I beat my body and make it my slave so that after I have preached to others, I myself will not be disqualified for the prize.

1 CORINTHIANS 9:26-27

What's missing in that? I don't hear in Paul that self-righteous smugness that says, "I've prayed the sinner's prayer, and I'm good to go from here on out." He said, "I exercise extreme discipline in my life, because I don't want to be disqualified after I've helped other people find their own way." There's an assertive nature in message after message to community after community that populates our New Testament. And it's the message for the Church in the twenty-first century.

You've all been to the stadium and seen the athletes race. Everyone runs; one wins. Run to win. All good athletes train hard. They do it for a gold medal that tarnishes and fades. You're after one that's gold eternally. I don't know about you, but I'm running hard for the finish line. I'm giving it everything I've got. No sloppy living for me! I'm staying alert and in top condition. I'm not going to get caught napping, telling everyone else all about it and then missing out myself.

1 CORINTHIANS 9:24-27 (THE MESSAGE©)

III. THE FORCES THAT DETERMINE HISTORY: VISIBLE AND INVISIBLE

If I had to put a bow around it, and I do, I think the above statement is a pretty good summary statement: The forces that determine history fall into two categories: visible and invisible. You watch the evening news, and you get heated up about the visible. How much time and energy and effort do you invest in spiritual things? Don't just say, "I believe in them." Think about what you do with them, if you believe they exist.

Physical health doesn't come from saying, "I believe exercise is valuable. I believe it's really good if you don't ingest more calories than you burn, because if you routinely take in more calories than your burn, you're going to get a little fluffy." Now you can know that, but unless you adapt your behavior to align with what you know, you're just going to be informed and fluffy.

For too long in the Church, we've thought information was the equivalent of an outcome. We have a consumer mentality. "Oh, I've heard that. I've read that. I know that." Well, I appreciate that you've heard it, and you've read it. And I commend you for investing the time to learn it. But the real question is this: Is there fruit in your life that suggests you have practiced it?

My Bible says that we'll know one another by our fruit, not by our diplomas. What we want to let happen in our lives is that there be evidence from our behavior, from how we spend our resources and invest our time, what we're aspiring to, what we're encouraging the people around us to aspire to, what we cheer for. It should be evident that the things of the Kingdom of God matter to us. As the Body of Christ, we can't just go out trying to collect people that are like-minded. We want to go out into the highways and byways and find people that say they don't know the Lord and help them become fully devoted followers. It's important. Yes, we intend for our church to grow. Yes, we want to reach into the community. Why else are we here?

Visible forces are obvious. The invisible forces, a little less so. But forces at work in the non-visible realm exercise a continuous and decisive influence on events in the visible realm. My Bible says that God raises up kingdoms and puts them down—that invisible forces impact the rise and the fall of nations.

For our light and momentary troubles are achieving for us an eternal glory that far outweighs them all. So we fix our eyes not on what is seen, but on what is unseen. For what is seen is temporary, but what is unseen is eternal.

2 CORINTHIANS 4:17-18

There's that tension again between time and eternity. It's a paradox. It says, "Fix your gaze on what you can't see." How do you do that? Do you have to look with something other than your physical eyes? It's about belief and faithfulness. It isn't that we do the extraordinary. It's that we do the ordinary extraordinarily well. I'm not looking for people to do extraordinary things. I'm looking for people to own what we would deem to be ordinary—godly men and women, godly husbands and wives—where you keep your word, where you do the next right thing, but you do it extraordinarily well. In almost every endeavor in life that I am aware of, excellence comes, not from some freakish set of gifts, but from an inordinate attention to the fundamentals and perseverance in the application of those things. If you're extraordinarily gifted and you ignore the fundamentals, you'll fail when the pressure's on. You can have average giftings but give extraordinary attention to the fundamentals, and flourish under great stress. Our light and momentary afflictions are achieving something for us. It takes tremendous faith to believe that. We need one another to do that. The Bible says we have to encourage one another daily. You won't make it by yourself.

A. IMPORTANT FEATURES COMMON TO BOTH REALMS

There are some important features common to both realms. Their effect is seldom limited to the individual. Spiritual forces seldom affect just you. Often it extends to families and collections of families, tribes, communities, entire nations. We've seen it over and over again. One of the challenges we faced as a nation from our inception is rebellion. You know, we were birthed from a revolution. It's interesting—that's our self-perception. If you read British history, even from the British perspective, the taxation without representation wasn't fair. There was a burden placed upon us by an insensitive leader, and we finally said, "Enough!" The majority of the citizens would have gladly yielded to the king with just a reasoned response. But we were birthed in a rebellion. Until this day, it's a spirit that we struggle with. We're not great at taking coaching. We call it in American history, "Rugged Individualism," and in the language of the toddler, "Me do it." And once those forces are released, they tend to continue from generation to generation until something happens to cancel their effects. It's kind of the spiritual equivalent of inertia: A body at rest will remain at rest unless it's acted on by an outside force, or a body in motion will remain in motion unless it's acted on by an outside force. You need a power to break that inertia. That's why we need the help of the Holy Spirit. He's not optional.

Whatever point in your spiritual journey you have cooperated with Him, be certain that you're putting it into practice in the routine of your life. If Spirit baptism is a part of your journey, don't look at it like a medallion on the wall or a merit badge on your chest. Spend time every day praying in the Spirit. If that's not been a part of your journey yet, we'll talk more about it in the last chapter. Wherever you are in your journey, put it into practice. Ask yourself, do I involve myself daily in spiritual things? If the answer is yes, how is that? What do you do on a daily basis that is an acknowledgment of spiritual things, and investment of yourself? How is the Holy Spirit consciously involved in my daily life? Am I aware of Satanic or demonic influence in my life—yes or no? It doesn't mean you're being oppressed or possessed, but in your sphere of influence, do you see anything that you could say, "That's probably got something that's not holy engaged there." That's just to help you kind of pull the curtain back. Be conscious of it, not accidental with it.

B. THREE SPIRITUAL CERTAINTIES

1. THE SPIRITUAL WORLD IS REAL

Either the spiritual world is real, or we should close the church. The spiritual world impacts your life—physically, emotionally, financially—in every way.

2. THE SPIRITUAL WORLD IMPACTS YOUR LIFE

If you haven't yet invited God into your finances, you're making a grave mistake. It's like not inviting God into your health. It's like saying, "Whatever happens, I don't want God helping me be healthy. I'm just going to eat vegetables." You want to invite God into your physical strength. You want to invite God into your financial strength. What are you afraid of? Are you afraid He's going to ask you to give? Because I have a feeling you're going to ask Him to bless you. So if that's a discipleship point for you, go ahead and take that step of faith. It will change your life. In the season of uncertainty that is unfolding in front of us—with the shaking throughout the earth—security is in nothing other than Almighty God.

3. YOU HAVE SPIRITUAL INFLUENCE

As a Christ-follower, you have spiritual influence. What are you using it for? What is the fruitfulness of that? Do the people that know you, know you as a person of faith? I say that with embarrassment; there was a season in my life when I didn't like being a pastor. I didn't like wearing the label. You talk about a conversation killer—it's awkward when you walk up to a group of people you don't know, and they say, "What do you do?" And I say, "I'm a pastor." Its particularly awkward if your church is in a tent—and it was at the time. They can't back away from you quickly enough. I wrestled with it, so I understand a little bit of that tension. But you want to be identified with Jesus. You want the people that know you to know you're all-in with Him—that if they'll give you half an excuse, you'll pray for them at the drop of the hat (and you carry several hats). You might say, "Well, somebody will be offended." You're right. Somebody will be offended, but somebody will be blessed. What a privilege.

I thank God for you. Christ in you is the hope of glory. I know you're walking through hard places. I know you are, because I know the Lord asks me to also. But He will bring us through. The one who called us is faithful. I love Hebrews chapter 12, verse 2—it says that He's the author and the perfecter of our story. The one that imagined our story is the same one that's going to complete it. He's going to keep writing chapters until I win. Hot dog! I like playing on that team.

PRAYER: Father, thank You. Thank You for Your Church. Thank You for a place where I can gather with others to worship You and praise You and where others will encourage me and where Your Word will be lifted up. Lord, gather those who are hungry and thirsting and searching for You. By the Spirit of the Living God, bring health to their bodies and opportunities before them and peace to their lives and breakthroughs in their families. I thank You that You're a God who delivers. In myself, I am weak and frail, Lord, and so easily distracted. I grow weary in doing good, but in You, Father, in You I can run through a troop and leap over a wall. I thank You that Your arm is not too short to work salvation or Your strength too small to bring deliverance, and I praise You for it. In Jesus' name, I pray and believe. Amen.

UNLEASHING THE POWER OF THE HOLY SPIRIT

WELCOME

There are some things I can tell you about the Holy Spirit. I've mentioned some of this before, but it's worth repeating. He will not embarrass you. He won't humiliate you. He won't make you do something you don't want to do. He won't override your will. He won't override your own conscious awareness, your own self-determination. He won't make you say something you don't want to say. He won't make you do something you don't want to do. You may have met people who said, "Well, I didn't want to do it, but the Lord..." No, He didn't. I won't engage in the argument; the Lord didn't make you do something. If God were going to make you do something you don't want to, He would have caused us all to stop sinning long ago. We've held some preconceptions about the Holy Spirit that aren't helpful. We've held some attitudes and fears that are irrational. Maybe because we've seen people do some bizarre things—some odd or strange things—and not have the courage to own it themselves, so they blame God. It isn't God. Don't argue with them, that's not fruitful. But you don't have to let your discussion or your personal journey with the Spirit of God be driven out of fear and the bizarre behavior of other people. That's not prudent. So today we want to welcome Him into our lives.

I want to look at 1 Peter:

> *Concerning this salvation, the prophets, who spoke of the grace that was to come to you, searched intently and with the greatest care, trying to find out the time and circumstances to which the Spirit of Christ in them was pointing when he predicted the sufferings of Christ and the glories that would follow.*

1 PETER 1:10-11

Peter is talking about the Hebrew prophets of the Old Testament here. He's talking about the Major Prophets—Isaiah, Jeremiah, Ezekiel and also the Minor Prophets—all of those names that inhabit the last books of your Old Testament. I think you and I imagine that if you're called as a prophet and your body of work makes it into the Bible, that there must be something so unique about you that God should just drop upon you some sort of fully developed message—that He'd give you some insight so profound, so powerful, that it would almost dominate your life. It would override your vocal apparatus and you couldn't help but speak it out and you'd have to be some special person that's not like us. So, here in this verse, did you note what he said? He said, "The prophets, who spoke of the grace that was to come to you, searched intently and with the greatest care." That means the message of the prophets wasn't just something that God forced upon them. It was something that emerged from their own life-choices. They searched intently and with great care in the Scripture that they had. And out of their desire, out of their longing, out of their intense effort—God met them.

I would like to deconstruct the notion that people who know the Lord are just people that got some kind of goofy gift. You know, they're wired up different than us. Like maybe you and me, we're wired up to be kind of ungodly, and we're just trying to figure out how to get across the line. Or maybe there are those people that God just made holy, and it's easier for them. They just enjoy it—like a spiritual endorphin—they enjoy saying no to ungodliness. Not true. The prophets, Peter said, invested themselves heavily in the things of God, and God responded to them. He will do the same for you.

Now lets go on to verse 11 of that scripture. It says that they were "trying to find out the time and circumstances to which the Spirit of Christ in them was pointing when he predicted the sufferings of Christ and the glories that would follow." The prophets lived hundreds of years before Jesus. They weren't contemporaries, so note that it says that "the Spirit of Christ in them." That means the same Spirit that was in them, pointing towards the sufferings of the Christ, was the same Spirit that was in Jesus. The Bible says the same Spirit that raised Jesus from the dead dwells in you and me. So when we talk about welcoming the Holy Spirit, we are welcoming the wisdom of God, the power of God, and the presence of God. That same Spirit is the Spirit we read about in the first verses of Genesis before God ever spoke a creative, authoritative word over this world. It says, "The Spirit of God hovered over the face of the deep." It dwells in you. That same Spirit of God communicated to Noah everything he needed to know to build a floating barn. He dwells in you. If God could help Noah be prepared for his generation, do you think His Spirit could help you and me be prepared for our generation? That same Holy Spirit provided the laser guiding system, of sorts, for a stone from a little shepherd boy's sling. His name was David, and He directed it towards the vulnerable point on the forehead of the mightiest warrior of his day—a Philistine giant named Goliath—and brought about a victory. That same Holy Spirit visited Mary—a Jewish girl, a teenager—in a little insignificant village of the northern part of Israel, and the story of the incarnation was launched. That same Spirit of God is available to you and me. Do you think it might be prudent to welcome Him into our lives? Do we think there could be a benefit? I suspect so.

I. KNOWLEDGE OF GOD
& EXPERIENCING GOD

I want to take a moment and talk with you about a contrast that I think we struggle with—the idea of the knowledge of God and experiencing God. I want to suggest to you that it's not an either/or; it's not like we have to choose. It's really a both/and. We want an increasing knowledge as we learn about God, but we also want to experience God in increasing ways. Far too often, we choose one or the other.

For example, in church world, we're pretty good at Bible studies, right? We write studies, we go to studies, and we invite our friends. I read once that a high percentage of people that attend church, if we have a choice between going to Heaven or a seminar on Heaven, we'd go to the seminar. I'm not opposed to learning; I've spent my life learning. I'm grateful for that opportunity. I don't want to diminish it, but I would remind you that Satan knows more about God than all of us collectively. He has seen the Kingdom of God in the fullness of its glory, but he hasn't chosen to cooperate with God. So the knowledge of God alone will not make you a more effective Christ-follower. We want to add to that an experience with God, a yielding to God and a cooperation with God. We have to live with the imagination that God will inform our life with experiences and not just with information. It's very, very important. We don't just want to hold theological definitions and biblical terms. We want to be a repository of experience with Almighty God. When you reject the Holy Spirit, when you limit the Holy Spirit—in reality, you're exchanging the presence of God for the knowledge of God by saying, "I'll be content just to know about Him," because it's the Holy Spirit that brings the power of God to bear by impacting your life-experiences. We need His help.

> *But God has revealed it to us by his Spirit. The Spirit searches all things, even the deep things of God. For who among men knows the thoughts of a man except the man's spirit within him? In the same way no one knows the thoughts of God except the Spirit of God. We have not received the spirit of the world but the Spirit who is from God, that we may understand what God has freely given us.*

> 1 CORINTHIANS 2:10-12

A. DOUBLE-MINDED

James 2:19 says,

> *You believe that there is one God. Good! Even the demons believe that--and shudder.*

> JAMES 2:19

So if you woke up this morning and said, "Well, I believe

there's a God." Good! You qualify at least to be a demon. We want to take the step beyond that into yielding and obedience and experiences on behalf of Almighty God. What a thought. The Bible uses the term *doubled-minded*, and it's still alive in our vernacular today. I think we think of double-minded as being somebody who's inconsistent—a little wishy-washy, maybe they flip-flop a little bit. But the Bible uses it in a bit of a different context. It isn't just somebody that's indecisive. To be double-minded has significant spiritual implications. In James 1, verse 8, it says,

> *A double-minded man is unstable in all he does.*
>
> JAMES 1:8

In chapter 4 of the same book, it says,

> *Come near to God and he will come near to you. Wash your hands, you sinners, and purify your hearts, you double-minded.*
>
> JAMES 4:8

If you're a little inconsistent in your spiritual life—if some days you want to please the Lord and some days you don't. Or some days you think maybe I'll cooperate and some days you're not so sure—I think we say, "Well I'm a little inconsistent," or "I'm still working on it." But I want you to hear how James characterizes it. He says to the sinners, "You need to wash your hands." And to the double-minded, "You need to purify your hearts." He said there's something impure that's found its way in there that's flourishing, that's growing, and you need to purify that. It's not helpful.

In Colossians, it says,

> *Set your mind on the things above, not on the things that are on earth.*

COLOSSIANS 3:2 (NASB®)

Set your mind on things above. The meaning is easily grasped, but that is so very difficult to do, isn't it? That's not easy for me; we live in this world. The Bible says we're in the world but we're not of the world. But I'm telling you, it is hard to keep your mind anywhere near the things of God. We have assignments, responsibilities and things pulling on us. We have appointments that push their way into our lives and needs that cry out for our attention. Yet Scripture says to set our minds on the things of the Lord. How can we do that? We need help. We have to have the desire.

Look at Romans chapter 8:

> *Those who live according to the sinful nature have their minds set on what that nature desires; but those who live in*

accordance with the Spirit have their minds set on what the
Spirit desires. The mind of sinful man is death, but the mind
controlled by the Spirit is life and peace; the sinful mind is
hostile to God. It does not submit to God's law, nor can it do
so. Those controlled by the sinful nature cannot please God.

ROMANS 8:5-8

It gives us a bit of a prompt. It says, "Those who live according
to the sinful nature have their minds set on what that nature
desires." Again, it's pretty plain language—he said if you live
according to your sinful nature. If you're wondering how to
identify if you're living according to sinful nature, here's how you
know: Your mind is filled with that stuff rather than the things
of God. Then it goes on to say, "But those who live in accordance
with the Spirit have their minds set on what the Spirit desires.
The mind of sinful man is death, but the mind controlled by
the Spirit is life and peace." That verse is a bit helpful. If you
willingly give place in your thought life to ungodly things, it says
it's death. It's destructive. It will diminish you. It's not a neutral
thing.

B. EMOTIONAL "FRUIT"— ATTITUDE

Ungodly thoughts and ideas and images all have access to our
minds. They come to every one of us. But what I want to talk
about is what you give your thoughts to—what you purposely

feed into your mind. I'm talking about what you watch, what you listen to, and what you think about. It could also be about the emotions that you give vent to—the emotions that you let grow and emerge that you fuel with memories and thoughts and life-experiences and the attitudes of others. What is it that fuels your thoughts and your emotions and the will of your life? Is it driven by things of this world? Is there any distinction between what you're thinking about and what somebody that makes no pretense about God thinks about? Do you actually spend time and energy with relationships and discussions and information and things that fuel a thought life about the things of God? You cannot pursue God mentally with a passive posture. Pursuit is intentional. It requires self-discipline, just as much as physical health does. It isn't just thinking about what I want to think about, when I want to think about it. It's saying there are some things I will not pick up; I will not give them a place on the inside of me. There are some emotions I will just not entertain; they're not helpful in this season.

In the book of Galatians, in the fifth chapter, the Apostle Paul gives a rather lengthy discussion about this type of conflict—this tension with that part of us that he says is earthly, carnal, sinful, Adamic—of the earth. They all describe the same thing—that part of us that tends towards ungodliness. We all have that side of us. Have you noticed? If you haven't noticed yours, you've noticed it in somebody you work with. But in contrast to that, Paul says there is the fruit of the Spirit. When you cooperate with the Holy Spirit, who is in you, something else emerges in your life. He says that you want to intentionally cultivate the fruit of the Spirit. Why would you do that? Jesus said that we'll know our faith by the fruit of our lives. Not by where we sit on the weekends or what's on our bookshelf, but by the fruit of our lives. Not even just by our words, but by the fruit of who we are—our character. This type of fruit will develop in our lives if we'll cooperate with the Holy Spirit.

Look in Galatians 5, in verse 22. It says,

> *But the fruit of the Spirit is love, joy, peace, patience, kindness, goodness, faithfulness, gentleness and self-control. Against such things there is no law.*

GALATIANS 5:22-23

For those fruits of the Spirit to emerge in your life, for them to increase in your life, it requires a cooperation with the Spirit of God. They're supernatural. They're not just an expression of your self-determination and the force of your character. We aren't hardwired for those things. It takes the Spirit of God within us. But they aren't just reflected in our minds, they aren't just informational. Being a gentle person doesn't mean you know the definition of gentleness. Letting gentleness emerge in your life is about an attitude. It's the way you interact with God and with other people. The same is true of patience or kindness or goodness. Most of the things in that list, from a secular vantage point, look like weaknesses. Yet God says against those things there is no law—nothing will supersede them if you cultivate them. If you care about them and desire them—if you want them to emerge in you, they will give you a better life. If I were responsible for causing the Church to become ineffective, inert, inactive, I would begin by trying to convince the Church to not cooperate with the Holy Spirit. Because if I could keep you opposed to the Person of the Holy Spirit, you'd remain in ignorance about the redemptive work of Jesus and the power of the Cross and the power of His shed blood. And the character of God would not emerge in you. But if we cooperate with the Holy Spirit, the character of God comes forth in us. Then, we become someone through whom the purposes of God can emerge more fully. He will help you. He will.

There's a tension in us. This isn't automatic. This is about being purposeful, and if you don't intend it to happen, it's highly improbable it ever will. In Matthew 6, Jesus said,

"Therefore do not worry about tomorrow, for tomorrow will worry about itself. Each day has enough trouble of its own."

MATTHEW 6:34

Can I get an amen on that one? Again, Jesus said it plainly. He said, "Don't worry about tomorrow. Just don't do it." He wouldn't have told us not to do it if He didn't know it was going to be a struggle. Life is challenging and difficult—Jesus said so. He said,

"Hey, in this world you're going to have trouble." It's not more or less easy if you are a Christ-follower. He is saying, "Don't let your life be filled with anxiety and worry and stress. It's not helpful." He's acknowledging that tension in us. He's saying, "You can deal with tomorrow when you get there." It's not a banishment of planning or preparation. He's simply saying don't borrow trouble you don't have today.

In John 14, Jesus said:

> *Peace I leave with you; my peace I give you. I do not give to you as the world gives. Do not let your hearts be troubled and do not be afraid.*
>
> JOHN 14:27

If Jesus said we don't have to be afraid, we don't have to be. I'm telling you, fear grips our world in an unprecedented way. We're afraid of the future. We're afraid of the past. We're afraid for our kids. We're afraid for our parents. We're afraid for ourselves. But Jesus said, "My peace I give to you." Now, you need to know a bit about Jesus' life. Jesus did not lead a life free of conflict. From His birth to His resurrection, His life was defined by conflict. Herod killed all the babies in Bethlehem where Jesus was born, anywhere in the birth range that he knew about. Mary and Joseph had to flee. Jesus' life was marked by antagonism, unfair criticism, rejection, all sorts of challenges. Until, finally, on a Roman cross He died. So when Jesus says, "My peace

I give to you," you need to step back for a minute. It's not an absence of conflict—what Jesus demonstrated for us was a calm assurance of God's unfailing presence with Him. You never see Jesus in panic mode. He's in a boat with a group of fisherman— He's the carpenter—and they get caught in a storm, and Jesus is asleep. They wake Him up to tell Him He's going to drown. What friends! But Jesus says to the wind and the waves, "Oh, be quiet," and it grew still. You never find Jesus frightened or intimidated—He knows that God is watching. He even says to Pilate, the Roman governor, "You've got no power over me." He said, "My Dad's given you a title, but you need to tread lightly." I mean, that's the "Living Bible," but it's basically what He said. "Don't make my Papa come for you. It will not go well."

"My peace," He said, "I give to you." You may think because there's turmoil, agitation, and conflict in your life that God has abandoned you. He hasn't. He's not angry with you. He isn't punishing you. He wasn't punishing Jesus. He's given you everything you need to walk triumphantly through that season. You may say, "Well, I didn't want to walk on this path." That's a different discussion. If we have our minds directed toward the things of God, even in the challenging, unpleasant and uncomfortable places, we can say, "God, I want to be sure I get Your purpose in this." It's a perversion of the gospel that says to be a Christ-follower means every day is a trip to Disneyland, that every meal the Lord serves you is a dessert buffet. It's not the truth, and we've got to grow up as the Church on that point, or we won't be able to fulfill what God has called us to in this season. We need the help of the Holy Spirit.

In Philippians it says,

> *Do not be anxious about anything, but in everything, by prayer and petition, with thanksgiving, present your requests to God. And the peace of God, which transcends all understanding, will guard your hearts and your minds in Christ Jesus. Finally, brothers and sisters, whatever is true, whatever is noble, whatever is right, whatever is pure, whatever is lovely, whatever is admirable—if anything is excellent or praiseworthy—think about such things.*

PHILIPPIANS 4:6-8

Do you have an imagination that your heart, mind, emotions, and will need guarding? If you've had the imagination, what's your protocol? You know how to guard your home. You know how to guard your children. You wouldn't put them in the car without appropriate protections. You know how to guard your investments. What's your daily protocol for guarding your mind, your thoughts, your emotions, and your will? It's important.

If there is a conflict in us—and we're trying to learn to set our thoughts on the things of God so that life can come to us—we have to acknowledge this tension. Well, in verse 8 we get some help. It says, "Whatever is true, whatever is noble, whatever is right, whatever is pure, whatever is lovely, whatever is admirable—if anything is excellent or praiseworthy—think about such things." It gives us a list, and it's a complex list. It doesn't say if something is only true, that you should think about it. It also needs to be noble and pure and trustworthy. You see, sometimes we get stuck on something in our head and say, "Well it's the truth!" But you can fill your heads with individual facts that are truth and still end up in a very destructive place. It's like saying broccoli is good for you. If all you eat is broccoli, it's not good for you. You'll turn green and smell bad. It doesn't diminish the truth that broccoli is good for you, but it's not intended to be the only thing you consume. And in our thought life we're given some direction for it. Do you have the maturity—are you willing to consider the discipline—to engage some filter on what you will give your thoughts to? It'll change what you watch and listen to. Once you start to own that idea, it will help you reorient the people you'll listen to. Some people you have to listen to because of assignments and life-responsibilities and day jobs. I get that, but with your discretionary time, there are some voices you could use less of, and there are some you could use more of. Guard your heart and your mind. The Holy Spirit will help you. He will.

II. OUR HELPER

Now I want to talk to you about this notion of the Holy Spirit as our Helper. When Jesus came to the earth, I believe there was a definitive purpose for His life. Would you agree with that? I think with just a casual reading of the Scriptures you would have the notion that Jesus' life was on purpose. It wasn't arbitrary or whimsical—He wasn't just hanging out and doing whatever. Jesus had a Kingdom-purpose for His life. Is that fair? I would submit to you that in equal measure the Holy Spirit is in the earth for a Kingdom-purpose. You believe Jesus came with a purpose that brought benefit to you. I would submit to you that the Holy Spirit is in the earth with a purpose of equal benefit to you. It makes no sense to limit your invitation to Him.

Listen to what Jesus said in John 16:

> *But I tell you the truth, it is to your advantage that I go away; for if I do not go away, the Helper shall not come to you; but if I go, I will send Him to you.*
>
> JOHN 16:7, NASB®

Jesus is speaking here and He said, "I tell you the truth." By now you've learned when you see that phrase in Jesus' teaching you know that what comes next is so bizarre that if Jesus didn't introduce it by saying, "I'm telling you the truth", you'd think He was making it up. So when you read that Jesus says, "I tell you the truth", lean in a little bit, because something really crazy is coming. Jesus said, "I tell you the truth, it is to your advantage that I go away."

I'm glad He said, "I'm telling you the truth," because that doesn't seem right to me. I'm thinking if Jesus rode home with me in the car, that'd be really good. And then He tells us why it's better if He goes away. He says, "For if I do not go away, the Helper shall not come to you; but if I go, I will send Him to you."

Jesus thought we were better off with the Holy Spirit than if He stayed. I believe Jesus told us the truth. It may be we have to recalibrate our attitude a bit.

A. KNOWLEDGE—REVEAL, MAKE KNOWN, DIRECT

Let's talk about some simple ways the Holy Spirit will help you. He'll bring knowledge to you—insight, understanding, not just information. He will give you understanding into who you are, how you're engaging the world, and how you can do it in a more godly way. The theological word we use for that may be *revelation*, but that sounds too spooky. But it's how to live your life with a God-perspective that will make a greater difference.

In Acts chapter 10 in verse 28, we get to listen in when Peter is speaking. He's in Caesarea. It's a Roman town on the coast of Israel. He says,

You are well aware that it is against our law for a Jew to
associate with or visit a Gentile. But God has shown me that
I should not call anyone impure or unclean.

<u>ACTS 10:28</u>

He said, "God has shown me." How did God show that to
Peter? Did he go to a Bible study? Did he get it when he studied
with the rabbi at the synagogue? The journey started a few days
earlier. Peter wasn't in Caesarea. He was in Joppa, which is an
ancient port on the coast of Israel that is still there today. It was
mid-day; he was waiting for the mid-day meal. He'd gone up
on the roof to pray. He had a heart for the Lord. He could have
been playing video games or doing some other thing to fill the
time, but he's on the roof praying, and he has a vision. He sees a
sheet let down from Heaven, and inside the sheet are all sorts of
things that he's not allowed to eat by Jewish dietary rule. And he
hears a voice that he understands to be God say, "Kill and eat."
He says, "Not me." And God said to him, "Don't call unclean
that which I say is clean." He sees that same scenario three times.
When it's done, there's a knock at the door down below. There's
a group of people standing there who aren't Jewish. And they
said, "We've come from Caesarea,"—which was a Roman pagan
town. They said, "We're looking for somebody named Peter. He
needs to come to our boss's house."

Now with the momentum of the vision, Peter says, "Well, I
shouldn't, but—maybe I should." It's a two-day walk to get

from where he was in Joppa to where they wanted him to go in Caesarea. I promise you, its two days of turmoil and anxiety: "What am I doing with these people? What am I going to do? How am I going to explain it? This is going to cost me something." He gets to Cornelius' house and Cornelius says, "You know, we really shouldn't be doing this. I'm a Roman Centurion and you're a Jew, so this isn't my idea to have you here, but I saw an angel. The angel told me where you were and how to find you, so I sent my guys to get you and now you're here. So, do whatever it is that you do." The next part was almost exactly like the events that happened in Jerusalem on the day of Pentecost when the Holy Spirit was poured out on Peter, James, John, and Mary, with Jesus' most trusted followers. That exact experience was duplicated in Caesarea on the non-Jews—on a Roman soldier and his household. What does Peter say in response to it? He said, "God has shown me…" He didn't read it in a book, and it wasn't a singular event. The Holy Spirit intersected his life and the lives of people around him, and it resulted in a significant shift in Peter's spiritual life. This is Peter that spent three years with Jesus. This is Peter that walked on the water. This is Peter that stood in the cemetery when Lazarus walked out. This is Peter that denied Jesus and was restored by Jesus himself. This is Peter that preached on the day of Pentecost and thousands of people accepted Jesus in a city that had previously rejected Him and were baptized in public. This is Peter that could point to his spiritual curriculum vitae and say, "I don't need to change anything. I'm the baddest boy on the block." He's standing in front of a Roman soldier and his household—Pagans—and he says, "God has shown me something. As much as I want to say that you're impure and you're unclean and you're second class, I can't say that to you."

Do you think from this example we might need the help of the Holy Spirit? Do you think it might be helpful to say to Him, "If there's any idea I hold that limits me, if there's any life-experience that I've had that could diminish me, if there's any pain I have suffered and the residual from that pain is limiting me, if there's any family system issue that's touched my life—help me, God. I don't want to be diminished. I don't want to miss what You've created me for. Help me." He will. That is such good news. He will give you insight and understanding. He may bring it in a vision, He may bring somebody else to you. There may be a knock. I don't know how it will happen, but He will.

But you have to want it. You have to care about it. Remember what we read earlier in Peter. Peter said, "The prophets searched intently with great care." Don't be casual with the Lord. Why would Almighty God, the Creator of Heaven and Earth intrude on your life if you don't want Him?

B. GIVES STRENGTH

Here's another way the Holy Spirit helps you; He'll give you strength—literal, physical strength. There are many biblical examples I could give you for this, but let's revisit the story of Samson. One of the things that's really consistent in the story is nobody that knew Samson could understand why he was so strong. So I don't think Samson looked like a gym rat. You know, he didn't walk around in muscle shirts making the rest of the people feel inadequate. Because when people looked at Samson, he didn't look strong or they would've all known why he was strong. I don't know if he was a diminutive little fellow or he was kind of fluffy. I don't know what he looked like, but he didn't look strong. He didn't, because he freaked out the enemy. They'd say, "How can that guy be so strong? What's his secret?" Then they went to enormous, elaborate lengths to find out his secret. If he'd been seven feet tall, four hundred pounds and could lift a truck, they would have known his secret. But they finally succeeded in having him betray his secret. They took Samson and they burned out his eyes and they put him into a life of public humiliation. This man of great strength—when his strength was gone—they made him grind grain like an ox or a donkey. They taunted him.

Now, in many respects Samson did it to himself. He'd lived a casual, sloppy, and immoral life. He didn't value the things of God. His God-story started before his birth with his parents and a commitment they made to the Lord and an invitation that God gave to Samson. It says the Spirit of God had come upon Samson and he would be able to accomplish things that he couldn't do by himself. Did you know God created you for things to be accomplished in your life that you cannot accomplish without His strength? You can't fulfill God's purpose and plan for your life in your own strength. If you're still endeavoring to serve the Lord just with your strength and your ability and your wisdom and your focus and your self-determination, you're forfeiting much of what God created you for. There's strength He would bring to you.

Finally, in the Samson story, they're having a celebration— they're gathered in a pagan temple, worshipping a pagan idol because they have been given victory over their great adversary, Samson. They send a child to bring Samson so they can mock him some more in public. They bring Samson in. And he says to the child that's leading him, "Could you let me rest on the pillar that holds this place up?" And listen to Samson's prayer. It's in Judges 16:

> *Then Samson prayed to the Lord, "O Sovereign Lord, remember me. O God, please strengthen me just once more, and let me with one blow get revenge on the Philistines for my two eyes."*

JUDGES 16:28

I think Samson's had a lot of days to think about his choices. I think he's had a lot of time. I don't hear anger. I don't really think it's a cry for revenge. I don't hear him mention Delilah. I hear him say, "God, could I feel that strength just one more time? I know what it was like when your Spirit came upon me.

I know I presumed upon it. I know I took it for granted. One more time, God?"

Now, I don't know, because we don't have a lot of detail in the scripture. But in my imagination when Samson begins to feel that strength burgeoning within him again, I see him start to smile. I think his last breaths were a belly laugh, because he knew God hadn't stepped away from him—that he wasn't abandoned.

Failure is not final. We need the help of the Holy Spirit. We have misunderstood, and we have stood at a distance with very limited invitations before us—very reluctant, more fearful than interested, more reserved than we have been enthusiastic. The Holy Spirit won't embarrass you. He won't humiliate you. He will help you. Jesus said that. Jesus said it was the best way for us to be here—and I believe Him. Jesus did what He could do on our behalf, and He sent His Spirit to help us understand the implications for ourselves that we might live lives not just with information but lives experiencing the power of God. It is time for the Church to be awakened and let it begin in us.

Here's a prayer you can pray. It's a prayer of invitation to the Holy Spirit. I want to encourage you to pray it. In fact, I want to encourage you to do more than that. If in the place you work there's another person that's a Christ-follower, get that prayer out and offer it as an invitation to the Spirit of God in the place of your employment. Do it quietly. Don't jump up on your desk, alright? In the neighborhood you live, if there's someone else that lives near you or around you that's a Christ-follower, take that prayer and pray it as an invitation to the Spirit of God in your neighborhood. Pray it for your city. Pray it for your state. Pray it for our nation. We need God's help, and I believe there's something powerful, profound and significant when the people of God extend an invitation to the Spirit of God to come into our midst. He will help us. It's a great opportunity.

PRAYER: Heavenly Father, I welcome Your Holy Spirit into my life—without any resistance. I need Your help. Apart from You, I cannot stand. Thank You for Your abiding presence, Your great power, and Your mercy. Give me an understanding heart that I may serve the Living God with joy and freedom. May Your life strengthen me today—body, soul, and spirit. In Jesus' name, amen.

AN INVITATION TO
SPIRIT BAPTISM

The Bible gives us some pretty simple categories for living life in the Spirit. It talks about being born of the Spirit, being baptized in the Spirit, leading a life that reflects the fruit of the Spirit, and the gifts of the Spirit. Those are the categories that I want to use to try to unpack this idea with you.

In Revelation chapter 1, John is writing and he says,

> *I John, your brother and companion in the suffering and the*
> *Kingdom and the patient endurance that are ours in Jesus,*
> *was on the island of Patmos because of the word of God and*
> *the testimony of Jesus.*

REVELATION 1:9

John is not on holiday or on a cruise with a day excursion—he has been exiled. It's the functional equivalent of being imprisoned, but rather than putting him in a building, they put him on an island. His peer group—including Peter and James—

have already been martyred. Most scholars believe John is alone by the time he writes the book of Revelation. He was the only one of the original group that Jesus recruited who wasn't martyred. And at the end of his life, he's been exiled to the island of Patmos. And he says in verse 10:

On the Lord's day I was in the spirit and I heard behind me a loud voice like a trumpet.

REVELATION 1:10

But before we go unpack the notion of being in the Spirit I want to be certain we don't miss the context in which that occurred. John said to us that he was our "brother and our companion." There's something electric in that to me. Can you imagine being a brother and a companion with one of the men that served with Jesus? He invites us right into the story to stand beside him, but he gives it a very specific context. He says he's our "brother and companion in this suffering and kingdom and patient endurance that are ours in Jesus."

Now we're going to focus our attention on what it means to be in the Spirit, but I want us to understand that this is John who experienced the supernatural ministry of Jesus and walked with Him. He interacted with the resurrected Christ, and had been faithful as a servant to Jesus for the decades of his life. And now, nearing the end, he describes his life as one of suffering, participation in the Kingdom of God, and patient endurance.

And from that context he said he was in the Spirit. It requires me to re-channel how I have thought about being in the Spirit. I had thought that to be "in the Spirit" meant that the problems of my life would melt before me. And I didn't arrive at that totally alone. I've spent forty years of my life or more in the midst of Christians having some dialogue about the Holy Spirit. And often those of us that inhabit podiums give the idea that to be "Spirit-filled" or to be "in the Spirit" means that you have the insight or authority or power that causes every obstacle to yield before you, so that you lead a trouble-free and victorious life— leaping from one mountaintop to the next.

Now I believe God brings victories and triumphs and mountaintop experiences to our lives, but if John finds himself as a prisoner and he describes his existence as embodying suffering and patience endurance, I would submit to you that you and I, being in the Spirit, Spirit-directed, Spirit-led and Spirit-filled, will not eliminate from our lives the need to endure and even suffer from time to time.

But if it doesn't eliminate the need to endure, why would we pursue a life in the Spirit? Because the alternative is a life in the flesh—a life that is limited to my strengths and my abilities. And I have some very real limits. When we participate with the Spirit of God in the purposes of the Kingdom of God, the opportunities of our lives are expanded exponentially. But it doesn't mean that those opportunities come to us without challenge or difficulty. John's life is making a difference in our world in the twenty-first century. How would you like to make choices in your life that would bear fruit for the Kingdom of God two millennia from today? I don't think you'll do that unless you learn to lead your life in the Spirit. So the value isn't necessarily ease in the moment—it is effectiveness for the eternal purposes of God.

So our objective in this chapter is to understand how you and I might find ourselves "in the Spirit." We know how to get in the church. We know how to get into the worship service. We may even know how to get into worship. But learning to lead our lives "in the Spirit" is a different kind of an invitation, and I'm going to suggest to you there's no singular answer to this. I've spent a lot of time in the Charismatic Renewal and the Pentecostal side of the Church, and there's a temptation to focus on a singular experience of saying, "That's what it means to be in the Spirit." And while I value those experiences, at this season of my life, I think leading a life "in the Spirit" has far more breadth than a singular experience. But what I'm inviting you toward repeatedly through this book is giving permission to the Holy Spirit to participate in your life without boundary. Don't begin the discussion by telling Him where He's not welcome and what you won't do. Because you need not worry—if He's not welcome, He won't bother you.

I. BORN OF THE SPIRIT

Being born of the Spirit is our entry point for the Kingdom of God. In John chapter 3, Jesus is speaking with a Jewish religious leader who's come at night. He's come under the cover of darkness intentionally. He doesn't want to be seen meeting with this itinerant rabbi in broad daylight, but he's hungry enough and intrigued enough and interested enough, so he comes to Jesus. And Jesus says to him,

> *"Truly, truly, I say to you unless one is born of water and the Spirit he cannot enter into the Kingdom of God. That which is born of the flesh is flesh, and that which is born of the Spirit is spirit. Do not be amazed that I said to you, 'You must be born again."*
>
> JOHN 3:5-7 (NASB®)

When Jesus said to Nicodemus, "You have to be born again," Nicodemus was perplexed. He said, "I'm an old man. That opportunity is impossible for me." And Jesus said, "I'm not talking to you about physical birth. I'm talking to you about the necessity of being born of the Spirit." Now that's a shock to a man whose entire life has been invested in the pursuit of religious rules—the food he eats, the holidays he celebrates, the way he orders his days, how he washes his hands—are all expressions of his faithful service of God. And Jesus has said to him, "Your rule keeping alone is inadequate. You need something supernatural to happen to you." And Nicodemus was astute enough and aware enough to recognize he was being presented with something that was beyond him. And I think the perplexity and frustration he felt was as much about the realization that his effort to keep the rules was inadequate as it was about the mystery of being born of the Spirit.

I take a moment with that because we have a tendency to be keepers of religious rules. You have some rules. And your rules aren't the same as everybody else's. But you have a sense of which rules you keep that commend you to the Lord. Now our life choices are a reflection of a desire to present holiness and purity to the Lord— we don't earn our way to the Kingdom. Sitting in church doesn't make you a Christ-follower any more than sitting in the garage makes you an automobile, or sitting in the gym makes you an Olympic athlete. So Jesus gave to Nicodemus the key: He said, "You have to be born of the Spirit."

In 2 Corinthians 5, it says that we become "a new creature." In Galatians 6, it says that neither circumcision nor uncircumcision makes any difference—what matters is the new creation. In Romans it says that we have to confess with our mouths and believe in our heart that Jesus is Lord and we'll be saved.

When you and I make a profession of faith in Jesus Christ, the outcome is a new birth—a spiritual birth. The same Spirit that brought Jesus back to life again brings about a transformation in us. We still have the same package—we're still in the same earth suit. We look the same. We have the same odor. But there is a new power at work within us. To be a Christ-follower is to be a recipient of a supernatural event, and the only doorway into the Kingdom of God is Jesus of Nazareth. We believe He's the Son of God. We believe that on the cross He died as a result of our ungodliness and our wickedness—our rebellion. We believe that He was raised to life again that we might be justified—that we might be the recipients of all the blessings due His perfect obedience.

Our participation in the Kingdom of God is the result of a supernatural event that is initiated by the grace of God on our behalf. It's not merit-based. We didn't earn it. We're not qualified for it. It's not about our IQ or our height or our physical gifts. It is an expression of the grace of God to any human being who will receive it. No matter how gross the sin of our lives, no matter how destructive our past may have been or how intransigent we may have been in our ungodliness—if we will come to the cross in humility and acknowledge our sin and receive Jesus as Lord of our lives, the Spirit of God generates a new creation within us. There's a new power—a new authority at work within us. We are no longer slaves to sin. There is an authority at work in us to bring deliverance, if we will cooperate with it. You will not

[handwritten margin notes: Agree; Who in their right mind would have the presence of mind to refuse this gift?]

overcome evil on your own. Your will is not strong enough. We need the help of the Holy Spirit to do that. And when we are born of the Spirit that's exactly what happens. When you are born of the Spirit, the scripture says that the Spirit of Almighty God takes up residence within you. It's one of the seismic shifts of the New Covenant—that God doesn't dwell in a building built with human hands, but that He indwells you and me. We are the temples of the Living God. The New Testament says,

> *Do you not know that your bodies are temples of the Holy Spirit, who is in you, whom you have received from God? You are not your own; you were bought at a price. Therefore honor God with your bodies.*

1 CORINTHIANS 6:19-20

Why do we honor God with our behavior? Why does purity and righteousness and holiness matter to us? It's an expression of honor to God for the price that has been paid so that we might participate in His Kingdom.

Before we move on, I want to be certain it's established in your heart that if you are a Christ-follower, the Spirit of the Living God is resident within you.

It's a significant shift from the worldview that we read about in the Gospels. When John came baptizing and calling the people to repentance, where did John baptize? In the Jordan River. It's at least a 20-mile walk from Jerusalem, into the desert. And the Jordan is not that spectacular. It's not the mighty Mississippi. So a 20-mile walk into the Jordan Valley from the city of Jerusalem to be baptized in the Jordan River is an expression of repentance.

On the day of Pentecost, when 3,000 people were baptized, where were they baptized?

All around the Temple Mount in Jerusalem there are mikvahs—religious spiritual baths; they look a lot like a stone hot tub—where the people would go and immerse themselves in water before they went onto the Temple Mount. So when those 3,000 people in the city wanted to be baptized, they didn't go to the Jordan River. They were baptized in those mikvahs all around the Temple Mount.

But John didn't invite people to that. He invited them to a very intentional directing of their attention away from the building of the Temple. Again, the Temple was the most remarkable building in all of Israel. It was the center of their life. It was the National Bank. It was the center of their political autonomy and their hopes for the future. When Jesus said, "If you destroy this temple, I'll rebuild it again in three days," they said, "You're crazy. It took 46 years to build it. What are you going to do?" So there's this mindset of turning the people's attention away from the Temple. And Jesus, at the very beginning of His ministry, says that it is what happens in you that's more important than what's happening on the outside of you. The disciples couldn't believe it. Jesus said, "Don't you know it's not what goes into your mouth that makes you unclean?" It's not a kosher diet. He said that it's what comes out of your mouth that makes you unclean. He's reorienting their lives. When you and I decide to follow the Lord, He's going to reorient your life. And you say, "I've been in church all my life. I've got the big rock ideas in place." Don't you think Nicodemus thought that? Don't you know that Saul of Tarsus thought that? And yet God brought significant redirection to them, did He not? I want to ask you if you have the humility to allow God to bring redirection to you. Let's say to the Lord, "I don't know it all, but I would like to learn." He'll help us if we will.

So with your profession of faith—a confession of faith, salvation, conversion, Kingdom-initiation—whatever label you use for that entry point into the Kingdom of God, the Spirit of God takes up residence within you. It's a supernatural event, but that's not all the Bible says about the Holy Spirit. For many of us, that's where our discussion stopped. We just decided we got it all when we were born again. Now I would agree with you—you get legal access to everything, but it doesn't mean that everything has become a part of your life experience or is at your disposal. When you are born in a physical body, you genetically have everything you need, but you haven't fully developed it or utilized it yet, have you? And when we're born into the Kingdom of God, we have been given legal access to the Kingdom of God in its entirety. But the reality of that has not yet become a part of our life experience. We have to grow up in the Lord in the same way we grow up physically.

II. BAPTIZED IN THE SPIRIT

In each of the four Gospels, Jesus is introduced to us in the same way. I want to focus on Matthew and John. In Matthew's Gospel, John the Baptist said,

> *I baptize you with water for repentance. But after me will come one who is more powerful than I, whose sandals I am not fit to carry. He will baptize you with the Holy Spirit and with fire.*

MATTHEW 3:11

And in John's Gospel,

> *I would not have known him, except that the one who sent me to baptize with water told me, "The man on whom you see the Spirit come down and remain is he who will baptize with the Holy Spirit."*

JOHN 1:33

All four Gospels introduce Jesus to us as the one who will baptize us with the Holy Spirit. That's not an accident. Very few of Jesus' miracles or life-events are recorded in all four Gospels, and yet all four Gospels introduce Him to us in the same way. So I would submit to you it's worthwhile in understanding what it means to be baptized in the Spirit or to understand Spirit baptism.

In John chapter 20, it's the evening of resurrection day. Jesus has been to the cross. It means His disciples have been with Him three years. They've seen Him betrayed, arrested, and beaten. They've watched the horror of a crucifixion, and they're hiding. They're afraid they're next. It says,

On the evening of that first day of the week, when the disciples were together, with the doors locked for fear of the Jews, Jesus came and stood among them...

JOHN 20:19

Were the disciples "born again" at this point in time? Hmm... so.

If they could crucify Jesus, they felt pretty vulnerable. Jesus could walk on the waves. He could command the wind. He conquered death. He called dead people from the grave, and they saw Him arrested, beaten, and crucified. You would feel like you had very few defenses, wouldn't you? So they're hiding. And Jesus came and stood among them. The last time they saw Him was on the cross, and now He's standing in the room.

"Peace be with you!" After he said this, he showed them his hands and side. The disciples were overjoyed when they saw

the Lord.

JOHN 20:19-20

That's an understatement. They freaked out, lost their minds—were overwhelmed.

Again Jesus said, "Peace be with you! As the Father has sent me, I am sending you." And with that he breathed on them and said, "Receive the Holy Spirit."

JOHN 20:21-22

Do you remember another place in the Bible where God breathed? Remember Genesis? It says God fashioned man from the dust of the ground, and He breathed on him and he became a living being. I don't believe it's an accident that similar language and imagery are being used in John 20. Jesus, on the evening of His resurrection comes first to His closest friends, and He says, "Peace be to you," and He breathes on them and says, "Receive the Holy Spirit." They've had a personal encounter with the resurrected Christ, and He's breathed on them and said, "Receive the Holy Spirit." It meets all the qualifications I know for the new birth. Would you admit them to fellowship in the Church at that point? I would. I don't know any criteria beyond that, that is necessary for them. They have already presented themselves for baptisms of repentance previously, so in John 20, on the evening of resurrection day, the disciples

Jesus' resur- rection is proof that God accepted His death on the cross.

experience conversion. Because until Jesus had been resurrected and glorified, that opportunity wasn't available.

You see, prior to Jesus' crucifixion, we lived beneath the grace of God. On the Day of Atonement, that the Jewish people celebrate on an annual basis, when they sacrificed an animal, God looked away from their sin in anticipation of the true sacrifice. The blood of an animal, the Scripture says, really was not satisfaction for the requirement of our sin. But God accepted the animal sacrifice in anticipation of the sacrifice of the Lamb of God, and Jesus met that righteous qualification. He offered His own blood, the book of Hebrews tells us, in the heavenly Holy of Holies. He sprinkled His blood on the Mercy Seat once and for all as a sacrifice for you and for me. And that resurrected Jesus meets with His friends and says, "My peace I give you— peace with God I give to you. Now receive the Holy Spirit." The disciples are born again.

In Acts chapter 1—Jesus spent forty days interacting from time to time with the disciples, but now He is going to return to Heaven. It's the ascension. And the narrative that leads us up to that in Acts 1 and verse 4, it says,

On one occasion, while he was eating with them, he gave
them this command:

ACTS: 1:4

You ought to circle "command." It's not a hint or a suggestion. It's a commandment.

> *"Do not leave Jerusalem, but wait for the gift my Father* *promised, which you have heard me speak about. For John* *baptized with water, but in a few days you will be baptized* *with the Holy Spirit."*

For repent-ance of sin.

ACTS: 1:4-5

I will establish a couple of things, because in the book of Acts they are significant. When you read a book by a single author, there is a consistent use of language. If you read books by multiple authors, they use words in different ways. Paul and James talk about faith in very different ways. It's not a contradiction; it's two people using language in a different way. But in the book of Acts, there's a consistency; we have an author telling a story. And in verse 4, Jesus said, "Don't leave Jerusalem but wait for the gift…" Circle the word "gift." "…that my father has promised, and you've heard me speak about. John baptized with water but in a few days you will be baptized with the Holy Spirit." The gift He's talking about is Spirit baptism.

In John 20, on the evening of resurrection day Jesus breathed on them and said, "Receive the Holy Spirit." We agreed a moment ago we would admit them into the fellowship of the Body of Christ—that they'd experienced the new birth—yet Jesus is commanding them to not even to consider beginning their

we did?

ministry until they process this baptism of the Holy Spirit.

So they met together and they asked him, "Lord, are you at this time going to restore the kingdom to Israel?" And He said, "It's none of your business." You know, they have an agenda and He has an agenda. It makes me smile. How many times do I say to the Lord, "Lord, do you see what I want you to do?" And the Lord says, "Uh-huh, do you see what I want you to do?" That's what's going on with the disciples. Jesus gives them a commandment, and they don't even ask Him a question. They say, "Mhmm, sure. Are you going to throw the Romans out?" And Jesus said, "It's none of your business. I love you, but it's none of your business." But then He refocuses them.

> *"It is not for you to know the times or dates the Father has set by his own authority. But you will receive power when the Holy Spirit comes on you; and you will be my witnesses in Jerusalem, and in all Judea and Samaria, and to the ends of the earth."*
>
> ACTS 1:7-8

He brings them back again to this participation with the Holy Spirit. You say, "Well I thought they received the Holy Spirit at conversion." On resurrection day, I believe they did. But Jesus very clearly is inviting them towards an experience beyond that. It's not about their birth into the Kingdom. We've already seen that birth in the Spirit takes place in their lives—He's inviting them into something else. The wording is different. The language is different. He's not telling them to be born again—He's telling them to be baptized in the Spirit. And they're not paying a great deal of attention, but Jesus gave them the purpose for Spirit baptism. He said, "You'll receive power to be my witnesses in Jerusalem and Judea and Samaria, and to the outermost parts of the earth." Those are expanding, concentric circles. Jerusalem is a city, Judea is a region immediately around it, Samaria is the next most outlying region, and beyond that is the outermost parts of the earth.

I had a class at Hebrew University with a very bright professor, and I remember a lecture he did where he used that passage. And he said he was convinced that to Jesus and his audience, beyond Jerusalem and Judea, Samaria was the outermost parts of the earth. I think we probably hold a little broader idea, but Acts chapter 2 is the fulfillment.

The disciples waited for 40 days. They didn't leave town. They didn't start their ministry. They waited. And in Acts chapter 2, it's the Day of Pentecost. That's not about being Pentecostal—Pentecost is a Jewish festival 50 days after Passover. It's a holiday. It's like saying, "on Easter Sunday" or "on Memorial Day," since Memorial Day is a few weeks after Easter.

When the day of Pentecost came, they were all together in one place. Suddenly a sound like the blowing of a violent wind came from heaven and filled the whole house where they were sitting. They saw what seemed to be tongues of fire that separated and came to rest on each of them. All of them were filled with the Holy Spirit and began to speak in other tongues as the Spirit enabled them. Now there were staying in Jerusalem God-fearing Jews from every nation under heaven.

ACTS 2:1-5

It's the holiday, there's a crowd in town.

When they heard this sound, a crowd came together in bewilderment, because each one heard their own language being spoken. Utterly amazed, they asked: "Aren't all these who are speaking Galileans?"

ACTS 2:6-7

To be a Galilean was the equivalent of being a hillbilly. Galilee was the remote—the rural. Jerusalem was the epicenter of activity. Galilee was more of a mixed population. Jesus referred to it as Galilee of the Gentiles.

"Are not all these men who are speaking Galileans? Then how is it that each of us hears them in his own native

language? Parthians, Medes and Elamites; residents of Mesopotamia, Judea and Cappadocia, Pontus and Asia, Phrygia and Pamphylia, Egypt and the parts of Libya near Cyrene; visitors from Rome (both Jews and converts to Judaism); Cretans and Arabs—we hear them declaring the wonders of God in our own tongues!" Amazed and perplexed, they asked one another, "What does this mean?" Some, however, made fun of them and said, "They have had too much wine."

ACTS 2:7-13

This is the fulfillment of the gift Jesus talked about in Acts chapter 1. Again, Luke is telling us a story. He wrote the Gospel that bears his name to tell us the story of Jesus' life and ministry. He wrote the book of Acts to tell us the story of Jesus' followers after His ascension. So Luke has a purpose in what he's telling. In the same way, you and I, if we're going to write a story, we would have an intent. He's not just pushing together pithy little sayings, or a collection of Jesus-events—he's leading the reader on a journey. In Acts chapter 1, Jesus says to His followers— He gives them a commandment—don't leave town until you receive the gift of the baptism in the Spirit. In Acts chapter 2, the Holy Spirit is poured out—that gift is delivered. And the outcome is that these Galileans—the ones you know—Mary, James, John, Peter, Andrew, and the crew, begin to speak in the languages that the visitors in Jerusalem recognize. So when we talk about speaking in tongues and praying in a language you don't understand, do I think it is gibberish? No, I think it's an earthly language. I think it's a language you didn't learn. It's not the result of the University or an academic course. I think it's an utterance given to you through the help and the influence of the Holy Spirit. Why? We'll get there.

But I want to draw your attention to the response. Some were amazed, some were perplexed, some were confused and asked one another, "What does it mean?" And some made fun. It occurs to me that two millennia later, when we talk about Spirit baptism and speaking in tongues, the responses are almost identical. Some are amazed. Some are perplexed and have questions. And some just ridicule. They accused them of being drunk. And Peter got up and said, "Nah, it's a little early for us. It's only nine in the morning. Four in the afternoon? Maybe."

Then Peter addresses the crowd. In Acts chapter 1, the disciples can't focus long enough to listen to Jesus. In fact, if you follow them through the Gospels, on more than one occasion Jesus looks at them and goes, "Are you really that dull?" And the answer would be, "Pretty much." In Acts chapter 2, following the Spirit baptism, Peter stands and addresses this crowd gathered in Jerusalem. You know the context—just a few days before this Peter wouldn't even stand next to Jesus. He said, "I don't know Him. I'm not one of his disciples." And now after the baptism in the Spirit, Peter is standing in the public square in Jerusalem, and he makes a masterful presentation of Jesus. What did Jesus say would happened in Acts 1:8? He said, "You'll be empowered to be witnesses for me." Peter hasn't gotten a PhD. He hasn't earned a new degree. He's been baptized in the Spirit. Here's the end of his lesson:

> *Therefore let all Israel be assured of this: God has made this Jesus, whom you crucified, both Lord and Christ.*
>
> ACTS 2:36

That's strong language.

> *When the people heard this, they were cut to the heart and said to Peter and the other apostles, "Brothers, what shall we do?" Peter replied, "Repent and be baptized, every one of you, in the name of Jesus Christ for the forgiveness of your sins."*
>
> ACTS 2:37-38

Let's stop there just a minute: "Repent and be baptized in the name of Jesus Christ and receive the forgiveness of your sins." Would you let them into the Church at that point? I would. Those are the markers I know for the new birth—for conversion. It's not a trick question. People said, "What do we do?" And the response was, "Repent and be baptized in the name of Jesus and your sins can be forgiven."

But he doesn't stop there.

And you will receive the gift of the Holy Spirit.

ACTS 2:38

Now if this weren't in Acts chapter 2 you might interpret that in many ways. But the gift of the Holy Spirit in Acts chapter 2, is inseparable from the gift of the Holy Spirit in Acts chapter 1. And Jesus wasn't talking to His disciples in Acts chapter 1 about conversion alone. He was commanding them toward Spirit baptism. The Holy Spirit is poured out in Acts chapter 2 and Peter stands up and addresses the crowd. They say, "What do we do?" And he says, "Repent of your sins. Be forgiven. And you can have the gift of the Holy Spirit."

[handwritten: Disagree]

Look at his next line:

[handwritten annotations: ① repent & be baptized in the name of J for forgiveness of sins · (This is an on the cross wasn't baptized) ② Or repent & be baptized speaking in tongues?]

"The promise is for you and your children and for all who are far off—for all whom the Lord our God will call."

ACTS 2:39

[handwritten: This suggests that all will speak in tongues. ???]

[handwritten: But later, Paul refers to tongues as one of the gifts not + other tongue gift in 1 Cor 12]

He didn't say this is a first century phenomenon. He didn't say this is a supernatural thing to get the Church jump-started. He said, "This is for everybody whom the Lord our God will call."

Again Luke is telling us a story about how to follow Jesus. In my opinion, Spirit baptism in the book of Acts opens the door to the supernatural life of the Church. Prior to Acts chapter 2, the disciples' response to Jesus was, at best, inconsistent. There

[handwritten: sounds right]

were times when Jesus would give them a block of authority and send them out and say, "Go out in my Name and do this." But for most of the time Jesus was at the center of their existence. And they brought their problems to Jesus, and He would resolve them. When the case was too difficult or the challenge was too great, Jesus would intervene and then He would look at His disciples and say, "Is your faith really so small?" And now when Jesus is ready to leave, He gives them a commandment not to leave until they're baptized in the Spirit. And then Acts chapter 2 happens, and on that very day 3,000 people in the city of Jerusalem, where they had orchestrated Jesus' crucifixion, acknowledge Jesus as Messiah and choose to serve Him as Lord.

Now as you read the book of Acts in chapter 3 and 4, Peter and John are on the way to the Temple to pray. In Acts 3, the lame man is healed. In Acts chapter 4, Peter, filled with the Spirit, addresses the crowd. In Acts chapter 5 we have Ananias and Sapphira. I mean, the church is rockin' and rollin' in Jerusalem—they're processing people by the thousands.

They had the gift of healing also.

I smile—we like to say the New Testament Church was a house church. It says they met in houses. But the church in Jerusalem in those early days wouldn't fit in a house.

In Acts chapter 5 Ananias and Sapphira lie—Peter says not to him, but that they have lied to the Holy Spirit. And they drop dead. It says the fear of the Lord came on the church in Jerusalem. When we talk about the Holy Spirit, and the moving of the Holy Spirit, and the power of God, and the supernatural— we want to very intentionally cultivate a reverence for God—a respect for God. It's not about self-promotion. It's not about elevating ourselves. It's not about our power. It's not about what we know. It's about the One that we know. We aren't baptized in the Spirit because of our degree of holiness or purity, or on the day of Pentecost the crowd wouldn't have been welcomed to the gift. Peter didn't tell them to go away and study for sixty days. He said, "If you will repent and choose Jesus you can be forgiven of your sins and you can have the gift of the Holy Spirit." It's not merit based—it's a gift. If it were merit based it wouldn't be a gift. Make sense? So if we're going to learn to lead a life in the Spirit, one of the things we want to keep crystal clear is that it isn't about us. It's about the purposes of God and the character of God. To Him be the glory and the honor and the praise and thanksgiving.

It is only by the gift (1 Cor. 12)

After the day of Pentecost there's this doorway into the supernatural. Acts chapter 7 is Stephen. Up to that point, Stephen's presentation of the gospel is the most remarkable we have. Stephen out-preaches Peter on the day of Pentecost. His presentation is so strong, so anointed, that it causes the enemies of Jesus to murder him in the streets. And before he leaves, it says he looked up and he said, "I see Jesus standing at the right hand of the Father."

III. THE BOOK OF ACTS

In Acts chapter 8 we get the second installment of what Jesus said in Acts 1:8. He said, "When you're baptized in the Spirit you'll be empowered to be my witnesses in Jerusalem." Jerusalem and Judea are synonymous. And then he said, "Then you'll be empowered in Samaria." In the next chapter it says,

> *Philip went down to a city in Samaria and proclaimed the Christ there. ... But when they believed Philip as he preached the good news of the kingdom of God and the name of Jesus Christ, they were baptized, both men and women.*
>
> ACTS 8:5,12

Sounds like people being born again. Sounds like an evangelistic service, doesn't it?

> *Simon himself believed and was baptized. And he followed Philip everywhere, astonished by the great signs and miracles he saw.*
>
> ACTS 8:13

Simon is a sorcerer, a magician—there's a false spirit in the community. All the way through the book of Acts you will find the true and the false flourishing simultaneously. It's no different in the twenty-first century.

The supernatural is intended to be an attestation of the presentation of the Gospel of Jesus Christ. Isn't that good to know? When the apostles in Jerusalem heard that Samaria had accepted the Word of God, they sent Peter and John to them. When they arrived they prayed for them that they might receive the Holy Spirit. Now if they have accepted Jesus, the Holy Spirit is resident within them. We've established that sometime back, but again, in the context of the book of Acts we're dealing with this commandment to be baptized in the Spirit, so when they hear that revival has come to Samaria, in come Peter and John.

> *Because the Holy Spirit had not yet come upon any of them; they had simply been baptized into the name of the Lord Jesus. Then Peter and John placed their hands on them, and they received the Holy Spirit. When Simon saw that the Spirit was given at the laying on of the apostles' hands, he offered them money...*

This indicates the Samaritans spoke in tongues.

ACTS 8:16-18

Jews ↑ to Samaritans ↓ Gentiles

Now, in Samaria, Luke does not say explicitly that they spoke in tongues, but something was happening to them that was so identifiable that Simon was offering money to have that power himself. So I would submit to you that what Jesus said would happen in Jerusalem and then in Samaria, is happening in Samaria. Luke is telling us a story.

In Acts chapter 9, Saul of Tarsus is recruited. Now remember in Acts chapter 10, Peter is invited from Joppa to Caesarea. He's invited by a Roman soldier. He's a Gentile, which is against all the rules. It would be functionally the equivalent of you getting an invitation to come to a strip club to preach the gospel. That's an awkward situation, right? Because we would all know you can't do that. That's not appropriate—nobody's going to believe it when you tell them. And that's precisely the circumstance in which Peter finds himself. But before the invitation was extended he's had a vision of a sheet let down from heaven filled with unclean things—things inappropriate for Peter to eat. You know the story. God says, "Kill and eat." And Peter says, "No." And God says, "Don't call unclean what I call clean." So off Peter goes to Caesarea. When he gets there he begins to tell his Jesus-story. He's getting good at this. And here's the outcome in Act chapter 10:

> *While Peter was still speaking these words, the Holy Spirit came on all who heard the message. The circumcised believers* [that's code for the Jewish believers] *who had come with Peter were astonished that the gift of the Holy Spirit had been poured out even on Gentiles. For they heard them speaking in tongues and praising God. Then Peter said, "Surely no one can stand in the way of their being baptized with water. They*

have received the Holy Spirit just as we have." So he ordered
that they be baptized in the name of Jesus Christ. Then they
asked Peter to stay with them for a few days.

ACTS 10:44-48

If you go back and read Acts chapter 11 there are more verses invested in Peter telling the church in Jerusalem what happened in Caesarea than there are in Acts chapter 10 telling us what happened in Caesarea. Peter says, "I had a vision." Cornelius sees an Angel. Everything about it is supernatural. Peter is washing his hands and he's saying I didn't do this. But the germane point, it seems to me, for the narrative that Luke is giving us, is a fulfillment of what Jesus said in Acts 1:8. Something started in Jerusalem and Judea. It extended to Samaria, and now it has made it to Caesarea up to the non-Jewish world. We're right on the cusp of the whole world. This is no longer a Jewish initiative. The experience of Acts chapter 2 has been replicated, just as Jesus said it would be, when he gave them the commandment to wait for the gift.

It doesn't stop there. When Paul begins his ministry, traveling the Roman world, he introduces us to those cities that populate the back part of the New Testament—Ephesus, Philippi, Colossi, and Thessaloniki.

It happened that while Apollos was at Corinth, Paul passed
through the upper country and came to Ephesus, and found

some disciples. He said to them, "Did you receive the Holy Spirit when you believed?" And they said to him, "No, we have not even heard whether there is a Holy Spirit."

ACTS 19:1-2

Sounds like a discussion we would have today.

And he said, "Into what then were you baptized?" And they said, "Into John's baptism." Paul said, "John baptized with the baptism of repentance, telling the people to believe in Him who was coming after him, that is, in Jesus." When they heard this, they were baptized in the name of the Lord Jesus.

ACTS 19:3-5

Again, we would admit them in the fellowship of the Church at that point I think.

And when Paul had laid his hands upon them, the Holy Spirit came on them, and they began speaking with tongues and prophesying. There were in all about twelve men. 2 gifts

ACTS 19:6-7

Twelve men is the threshold you need to establish a synagogue—that's the tipping point. And again the events of Acts chapter 2 have been duplicated in Ephesus. What Jesus said has been literally played out in the narrative that Luke is recounting to us—in Jerusalem, Judea, Samaria, and into the outermost parts of the Earth. To the Gentiles and to the Romans (who are the oppressors) and then to the Ephesians—the Gentiles living beyond the land of Israel. And the pattern hasn't stopped to this day. It's happening in cities, counties, states, and nations. The Spirit of God is moving amongst His people. Now that's the narrative as Luke tells it. I'm giving you the short version.

IV. GOSPEL OF JOHN

Let me give you the Gospel of John. I think it's noteworthy. We look to John 20 to see resurrection day and Jesus breathing upon the disciples. In the same way that Luke's narrative tells you a story, John's Gospel tells you a story. John is taking the reader and inviting him on a very intentional journey to help you become a follower of Jesus. We read a moment ago in John 1 where John describes Jesus as the baptizer in the Holy Spirit. Well in John 4, Jesus is having a discussion with a Samaritan woman at the well. Remember the story? He says, "Go call your husband," and she said, "I have none," and He said, "Well, that's true, but you've had a handful and currently the man you're living with you're not married to." And the woman says, "I perceive you're a prophet." And so they enter into this dialogue about water. She's drawing water—it's a work assignment each day. And Jesus said, "If you knew who I was, you'd ask me for water," and she said, "Well, I'm up for that."

Jesus answered, "Everyone who drinks this water will be
thirsty again, but whoever drinks the water I give him will
never thirst. Indeed, the water I give him will become in him
a spring of water welling up to eternal life."

JOHN 4:13-14

What's Jesus talking to her about? It's the new birth. Something welling up to eternal life—isn't that what the new birth is about? Isn't that what we mean when we talk about being born of the Spirit? Remember, John writes the Gospel after Jesus ascended to Heaven. After it's all been lived out, John sits down to put the story to paper so that it's not lost. So again, it's not a random telling. He's inviting us on the journey, and he meets this Samaritan woman and Jesus invites her towards eternal life. Isn't that the new birth? There is no eternal life without being born of the Spirit. Haven't we agreed upon that? He's not inviting her to keep kosher rules. He's not inviting her to reject her Samaritan holidays and embrace the Jewish ones. He's inviting her towards eternal life.

In John 7, it says,

On the last and greatest day of the Feast, Jesus stood and
said in a loud voice, "If anyone is thirsty, let him come to me
and drink. Whoever believes in me, as the Scripture has said,
streams of living water will flow from within him." By this
he meant the Spirit, whom those who believed in him were

later to receive. Up to that time the Spirit had not been given,
since Jesus had not yet been glorified.

JOHN 7:37-39

Verse 37 and 38 are historical. They're a description of what happened when Jesus was on the Temple Mount at the feast. He said, "If anybody's thirsty…" Everybody in Jerusalem is thirsty—it's a desert. It's an E.F. Hutton moment. He said, "If anyone is thirsty…" Everybody leans in. And He said, "Let them come to me and drink and streams of living water will flow from within him." It's a different image than what He used with the woman at the well. He's not talking about something welling up to eternal life. Now He's talking about streams of water flowing from within you. And then John gives us an explanation in the next verse. Again, this is written after the fact. John is writing with the understanding he has post-Pentecost: "By this Jesus meant the Spirit, whom those who believe in him were later to receive. Up till that time the Spirit hadn't been given, since Jesus had not yet been glorified." My opinion—John 4 describes for us conversion, and John 7 describes for us Spirit baptism.

In John 16, Jesus is preparing His disciples for His exit. He says, "I'm leaving you, and where I'm going you can't come." And there's a great deal of angst and anxiety. Jesus is doing His best to prepare them. He said,

But I tell you the truth: It is for your good that I am going

away. Unless I go away, the Counselor will not come to you;
but if I go, I will send him to you.

JOHN 16:7

Same chapter, verse 12:

"I have much more to say to you, more than you can now
bear. But when he, the Spirit of truth, comes, he will guide
you into all truth. He will not speak on his own; he will speak
only what he hears, and he will tell you what is yet to come."

JOHN 16:12-13

Clearly he's talking about more than just conversion. He's
not talking about just getting your ticket punched to go to
Heaven. He's not just talking about new birth. He's capable of
describing that. He said to Nicodemus, "You have to be born
again. You have to be born of the Spirit." But now He's coaching
His closest friends and followers, saying, "If I go away, there's
another counselor coming to you and he'll give you insight and
understanding and revelation. He'll make known what you
need to know in the moment." Isn't that what you read about in
the book of Acts? Aren't the disciples fundamentally different
in the pages of the book of Acts than they are in the pages of
the Gospels? I believe they are, dramatically so. And I think
unfortunately we've been invited to a limited understanding.
We've been invited to the new birth, to birth in the Spirit. And

[handwritten margin notes: Don't agree. But Scripture isn't clear to me about this. After the Spirit settles on them, they're different. Until then, they are hiding in the upper room.]

at that point, we've kind of lost our focus or lost our interest. We've wanted to argue we've experienced everything.

And from my vantage point, to do that, we have to ignore many of the commandments and invitations of Scripture, because Jesus didn't stop in John 20 on resurrection day with the disciples. He gave them a commandment to come forward. Spirit baptism, as I understand it, is an experience subsequent to conversion. The only prerequisite is conversion, where the believer in Jesus can be baptized in the Holy Spirit. The evidence of that, we're given in Scripture, is speaking in tongues.

Therein lies the rub. If Jesus had said, "When you're baptized in the Holy Spirit, you'll eat M&M'S®, it would be a low threshold of discussion. We'd just have pockets filled with chocolate. But when He said, "You'll speak in tongues," it creates all sorts of points of discussion. I don't know why. I'll give you my opinion.

In the book of James it says that the most unruly part of our body is our tongue—that if a man can control his tongue, he's perfect. Most of us, as we grow and mature, learn enough self-discipline that we don't push and shove and bite and pull like the preschoolers. But we still launch assaults with our words. If I hit my thumb with a hammer, "Praise the Lord" may come out and it may not. I'm in process. So when we cooperate with the Holy Spirit and we yield the most unruly part of ourselves to the direction of the Holy Spirit, it's a point of yielding to the Lord. So it's not a surprise to me that God chose to associate speaking in tongues with Spirit baptism.

"Do I have to speak in tongues to go to Heaven?"

No. Period.

"Do I have to speak in tongues?"

No. But you can. ?

"Well, I have the baptism in the Holy Spirit, and I don't speak in tongues."

Thy 1 Cor.12 — Tongues is one of the gifts.. Some have it, some don't. Depends on θ, the given of gift.

Okay. I just can't support it from Scripture. I don't want to argue. I'm not trying to convince you I'm right. I'm just inviting you toward what I understand from the Word of God. When we're willing to allow the Holy Spirit to direct our prayer life, the scripture says we allow the Spirit of God to make intercession through us in accordance with the will of God. I can't tell you how valuable that has become in my life.

There was a time I probably thought I was bright enough to pray my way toward God's victory on Planet Earth. I assure you, I have arrived at a point in my life where if I receive the next three things I ask the Lord for, I'll mess it up. When I pray for you, I pray in the Spirit, and then I pray with my understanding. Because even if I knew you would receive the first thing I prayed for you, it's highly improbable I would ask for the right thing. But I trust the Holy Spirit to make intercession for you, *so do I* in accordance with the will of God. What did Jesus say? He'll

Disagree

I ask that God provide whatever "x" needs for the day. He knows. I don't need tongues to be sure I'm praying in His will.

make known to you all things. "You'll be empowered to be witnesses for Me."

Now another point of confusion that sometimes surfaces around the topic of Spirit baptism is the discussion in 1 Corinthians. There's a listing there of these manifestations—these gifts of the Spirit—two of which are speaking in tongues and the interpretation of tongues.

The Corinthian church was a raucous, immoral place. And Paul is seeking to bring some order to the Corinthian church, so he's talking to them about how to let that be practiced in the congregation. The baptism in the Spirit, as I understand it, is not about the public congregation. It's a personal, private prayer language where you choose to cooperate with the Holy Spirit in the privacy of your prayer life and allow the Holy Spirit to make intercession through you.

Sometimes we've been coached to be afraid. If we hear someone praying an unknown language quietly next to us, we'll say they were out of order because they weren't interpreting. Well, I've overheard people praying in English, and I didn't think they were out of order. Again, it's not to draw attention to ourselves. It's not a spiritual merit badge—that you've achieved some heightened state of spirituality and God has rewarded you with Spirit baptism. It's available to any believer who will ask.

Some of the most carnal Christians I have ever known speak in tongues. I give you that as a caution, because people will come to me and say, "Well, I knew so and so, and they said they spoke in tongues and they were wicked." And I'm like, "Very well could be." But it's an erroneous conclusion you've reached, because then they'll say, "Well, I don't want anything to do with it." It's the same argument that people say, "I knew so and so that said they were a Christian, and I know they were a hypocrite, so I don't want to be a Christian." Why would you miss out on the Kingdom of God because so and so was a hypocrite, and why would you miss out on participating with the Holy Spirit because somebody you encountered was inconsistent? It's a logical flaw. If Jesus provided for me a Helper, I'm going to get in that line.

Now praying in the Spirit, in my life, has been similar to learning to pray in any other language. When you begin, it's awkward. I've had the privilege of learning three or four languages, in academic settings, and it's a very humbling thing. I took Hebrew at Hebrew University. It was an immersion class. It meant from day one, no English. And I knew no Hebrew. I didn't know the alphabet. The first time the teacher spoke to me in English was when she asked me how old I was. I told her, and she thought I couldn't count. But the first time she called on me to say my name, I stood up in class and said, "I'm a pizza." There's just a lot of anxiety in using words that don't make any sense to you, and you're trying to think your way through it. Learning languages is easier for the children. They don't have the embarrassment or the shame. How many times do they ask you what something is, and you repeat it? Then they ask you again and you repeat it. But they're incredible learners, and in the same way we learn to cooperate with the Holy Spirit.

So there are some barriers you have internally. You think, *I'm making it up*, or, *this seems childish*. Learning any language seems childish.

There's a letter in Hebrew—Kchet. In the part of the world I grew up in, kchet is not a letter—it's a provocation. In the Middle East, it's a letter. I had to be convinced of that before I would break that one out in public.

When you pray in a language that is not intellectually fruitful for you, there are some emotional triggers. It seems childish. It seems unrealistic. I would submit to you it is an expression of faith.

Here's my conclusion. If I'm doing it with a pure heart as a part of my private devotion with the Lord, even if I were making it up, I don't think that's offensive to the Lord. Have you ever had a child write a card for you with crayon and pretend to put words on it? And when you looked at the writing, it was nonsense. Did you look at him and say, "My child is an idiot." No, I bet there was a hug and a reward involved. Right? I believe the same is true with the Lord. From the invitation of scripture, Jesus said, "If you ask me for a fish, I won't give you a scorpion. If you ask for bread, I won't give you a stone." So I believe if you ask the Lord to baptize you in the Holy Spirit, He will. Jesus is the baptizer. Isn't that what all four Gospels said? That if you ask him to baptize you in the Spirit, He will. And then you have the privilege of praying in your prayer language. Again, it's private. It's not for the public consumption. It's not for the congregation.

I believe there is a public place for those expressions of the Spirit, but that's not what I understand Spirit baptism to be. I think it's highly improbable you'll ever participate in the gifts of the Spirit if you're not willing to participate in the baptism of the Spirit. There is a sequence in the way it's presented. Before they got all the supernatural activity of the Church, Jesus commanded them not to even start until they were baptized in the Spirit. I don't believe Jesus was being flippant. We don't dictate to God how we will participate with Him. We receive the gifts He gives to us. And as we accept those gifts, He will entrust to us greater opportunities. If we reject those gifts, why should He entrust something else?

Again, the baptism in the Holy Spirit, as I understand it, is an experience subsequent to salvation, whereby God baptizes a believer in His Spirit. The Spirit of God comes upon us, and we're empowered to pray in a language that we don't understand.

Now God will not violate your will. He's not going to make you make a noise. That would be scary. People say, "Well, I prayed for the baptism and nothing happened to me." Folks, if God occupied you and vocalized through you, that would be scary stuff. You have the control when you pray in your prayer language just like you do when you pray in English. It isn't that God takes over your vocal capacity and forces sounds out of you. You have to be willing to make those sounds.

When I received the baptism in the Holy Spirit, an Episcopal priest prayed with me. It was in the sixties, and I remember where I was. We sat at a kitchen table in a friend's home, and he opened his Bible and explained it to me. And then we knelt in the floor and he said, "I'm going to pray in my prayer language. Why don't you just follow me?"

Now I was a child. You could say he was manipulating me, I suppose, if you want to be a skeptic. But I understood he just put an invitation in front of me. You can't follow me in a language you don't know. But if you will ask the Father, He will baptize you in the Spirit, and you can pray in your prayer language.

After having spent decades amongst charismatics and Pentecostals, I've noticed we want to collect Spirit baptism like a trophy and put it on the shelf.

"Do you have it?"

"Oh, I've got it. What about you, do you have it?"

"Oh, yes. I have it."

Folks, having it is not the objective. Using it is the objective.

It doesn't take me long in prayer to come to the end of what I know. We need a revival in our nation. Is that fair? But beyond saying we need a revival, do you know how to get it? I don't. So I pray in the Holy Spirit, and then if the Lord gives me an idea, I will pray with my intellect, in English, as fully as I know how. But I'm dependent upon the leading and the help of the Holy Spirit. Otherwise, I'm limited to Allen, and that is a really tiny little pool.

I think I've given you enough that I can pray for you to receive. Would you like to receive the baptism? I'm here to tell you, if Jesus has something for me, watch me get in that line. I am unashamed, unreserved, and enthusiastic. "What will people say?" I couldn't care less. They're going to talk about you either way. That's the truth. People said when I became a Christian, "Oh, you're making it up." I didn't get a laminated certificate in the mail, I just knew I said a little prayer, and the Bible said something supernatural happened to me. And I said, "Well, let's go." It's changed the whole trajectory of my life. The same is true of Spirit baptism. If you will receive it by faith it will change the trajectory of your life.

"Well, do I have to?"

No. If you don't want to, God has given you the power to choose. In fact, if you are just casually interested, you wait. I mean that with all sincerity. The only people I really want to pray for are the people that feel like if you are not baptized in the Spirit there's something missing in your life. I want you to know God has put an invitation in front of you, and to reject it means there's a consequence. If you're not there, wait.

PRAYER: Father, I thank You for Your Word—for its truth and power and authority. Lord, I want to be pleasing in Your sight. And I pray that You will open my heart to those invitations You have for me, that I wouldn't miss what You have for me. Lord, give me Your leading and Your guidance, in Jesus' name. Amen.

The only prerequisite I know is conversion—that you're a believer in Jesus Christ. So just to be certain that we've taken that step of faith and we all know it, I always like to make a profession of faith with somebody that wants the baptism in the Holy Spirit, because what we first want to know is we've been born of the Spirit. And that's not about a church or any other label. That's about being born again.

So let's just say a prayer together. As much as anything, I want you to know how to help somebody else. You can repeat this little prayer with me:

PRAYER: Almighty God, I'm a sinner, and I need a savior. I believe Jesus is Your Son, that He died on a cross for my sin, and that You raised Him to life again that I might be justified. Forgive me of my sins, and I forgive anyone who has sinned against me. Jesus, be Lord of my life. I want to honor You with all that I am and all that I have, in Jesus' name. Amen.

Born of the Spirit—a new creation in Christ. There's nothing like it. It changes everything. Now Spirit baptism, as I understand it, is just part of the equipment. It's a part of the tools. Jesus thought Peter and James and John and Mary and Martha needed to be baptized in the Spirit. I'm thinking He thinks we might benefit.

"Can I be a Christ-follower and not be baptized?"

Yes. Can you play football without a helmet? For a play or two. But it limits your effectiveness. Right?

So, we're simply going to ask the Father to baptize us in the Spirit, and at that point, you'll have to be willing to make the sound. Oftentimes—I've seen exceptions. I've seen people receive powerful, full languages when they were baptized in the Holy Spirit. But the more normal process is people tend to receive two or three words, much like we learned to talk. Right? Have you ever been around parents with their first child? The child chokes, and the mother swears she said, "Mama." The child was choking, but mama interpreted it to mean something.

I think when you and I, in response to a sincere request in faith, are willing to make that sound, God receives it with that same joy. I encourage you to pray aloud—whatever word, whatever sound would come to you—you take that step of faith. I can almost assure you—you'll feel silly, a little childlike. That's when we learn best.

"What if I'm making up?"

What if I am? My friends, when I got saved, said I was just pretending like I was better. No. I'm still just boring Allen.

Now again, what's the benefit? We're cooperating with the Spirit of God. We want to learn to lead our lives in the Spirit. You participate in baptism because God directed us toward it. So we're going to participate in Spirit baptism because God directed us towards it. We'll ask God for what He told us we could have.

PRAYER: Father, I read in Your Word where You said that I would be baptized with Your Spirit. And I come in obedience to that scripture and ask that You would baptize me in a powerful way with Your Spirit. I thank You for it. I want to yield my life to You. I want to yield myself to You without reservation—without limit, without preconditions—that Your purposes might come forth in me in this generation. Now give me a mighty baptism, in Jesus' name. Amen.

That's it. You don't have to feel something. You don't have an electric jolt down your spine. You know, people say to me, "When I got saved, I felt something warm from the top of my head to the soles of my feet." I didn't. I just said a prayer. My life was a response of faith. I don't think you have to have a feeling. Some people get one. God bless them. That didn't happen to me. And you don't have to feel something spectacular. You have to be willing to respond to the Lord.

If you prayed that sincerely, I believe God has baptized you in His Spirit. And that if you're willing, you can pray in your prayer language. So at home, at work, while you're driving, wherever you are, you stay open to that. You make whatever sound you feel like is in your heart.

I had a friend. He was a physician, and he was a very, very logical kind of a person. That's why he was my friend. And he wanted the baptism in the Holy Spirit. He prayed and nothing happened. And his wife got it, which really annoyed him. And he prayed and nothing happened. Then his daughter got it, which annoyed him even worse. And then his mother-in-law got the baptism. This went on for a period of months, and he finally said one night that he drove home, and he said to the Lord, "I'm not getting out of my car." He didn't know what else to do. He said he took the first consonant in the alphabet, with the first vowel sound. And he said he started through the alphabet. He took the first vowel sound with every consonant in the alphabet: "Baa-caa-daa." He said he got about six or eight consonants into his little progression until he knew the Lord had given him a prayer language.

You be willing to speak. Okay? You can start, and you can stop. If it's two words, you take that as a gift from the Lord, and you use them. Take time every day. Take ten minutes a day this week and pray in your new prayer language.

PRAYER: Lord, I thank You that You give me what I ask for, and I thank You that You're setting me free to pray in new ways, to cooperate with Your Spirit, that You're bringing new freedom and new liberty to my life, Lord, to use me in more powerful ways than I've ever imagined possible. Give me a freedom to pray as I've never prayed before, in Jesus' name. Amen.

NOTES

NOTES

NOTES

NOTES

NOTES

NOTES

NOTES

NOTES

ONE-YEAR DAILY DEVOTIONAL

STANDING FIRM

It's impossible to avoid the shaking that life brings. It's only by anchoring ourselves in the immovable things of God that we can be truly stable—able to stand when the storms come. This book is a tool for you, giving you a moment each day with Scripture and prayer. Use it alongside your Bible-reading time, or look up the daily Scripture in your Bible to find the full story. Resolve to intentionally know God through His Word better today than you did yesterday. He will be a firm foundation for you in every season.

THREE-VOLUME SMALL GROUP VIDEO STUDY & GUIDE

THE WHITEBOARD BIBLE™

The Bible tells a story, and these small group studies will help you more fully understand it. The three volumes of *The Whiteboard Bible* develop a twelve-point timeline that serves as the framework for all the characters and events in the Bible, beginning with Creation and concluding with Jesus' return.

For more from Allen Jackson—including sermons, books, and
small group materials—visit:

allenjackson.com

ABOUT THE AUTHOR

Allen Jackson is passionate about helping people become more fully devoted followers of Jesus Christ, who respond to God's invitations for their life.

He has served World Outreach Church since 1981, becoming senior pastor in 1989. Under his leadership, WOC has grown to a congregation of over 15,000 through outreach activities, community events and worship services designed to share the Gospel.

Through Allen Jackson Ministries™, his messages reach people across the globe—through television, radio, Sirius XM, and online streaming. His teachings are also available in published books and other resources.

With degrees from Oral Roberts University and Vanderbilt University, and additional studies at Gordon-Conwell Theological Seminary and Hebrew University of Jerusalem, Jackson is uniquely equipped to help people develop a love and understanding of God's Word.

Pastor Jackson's wife, Kathy, is an active participant in ministry at World Outreach Church.